BY THE
block
18 surprisingly simple quilts

Siobhan Rogers

DEDICATION

To my Mum and Dad—thank you for my childhood.
August 3, 2014

ACKNOWLEDGMENTS

I have many to thank for their help in creating this book,
including Aurifil Threads, Moda Fabrics, Michael Miller
Fabrics, Bernina Australia, Kim Bradley, Krista Withers,
Angela Walters, and Allison Korleski. A special thank-
you to my very patient husband, Matt—way back in our
photography class, who would have thought we would
end up with four children and quilts all over our house?

EDITOR Valerie Shrader
TECHNICAL EDITOR Rebecca Kemp Brent
ASSOCIATE ART DIRECTOR Charlene Tiedemann
DESIGNER Brass Bobbin Creative LLC
ILLUSTRATOR Missy Shepler
PHOTOGRAPHER Joe Hancock
PRODUCTION DESIGNER Katherine Jackson

 Interweave
A division of F+W Media, Inc.
4868 Innovation Drive
Fort Collins, CO 80525
interweave.com

Manufactured in China by RR Donnelley Shenzhen.

Library of Congress Cataloging-in-Publication Data

Rogers, Siobhan.

By the block : 18 surprisingly simple quilts / Siobhan Rogers.

pages cm

Includes index.

1. Patchwork—Patterns. 2. Patchwork quilts. 3. Quilting—Patterns.

I. Title.

TT835.R635 2015

746.46—dc23

2014033112

ISBN 978-1-62033-676-2 (pbk)
ISBN 978-1-62033-677-9 (PDF)

10 9 8 7 6 5 4 3 2 1

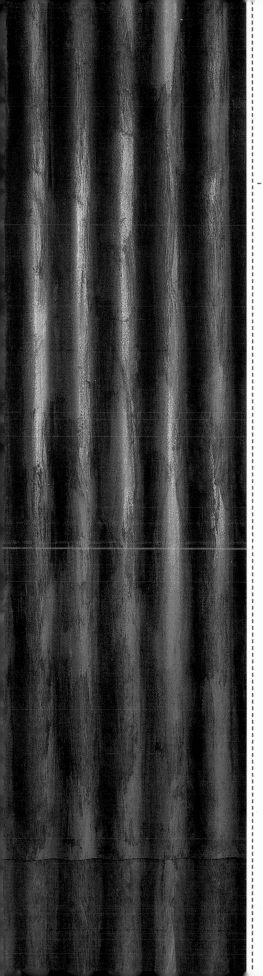

Contents

Introduction

I'm a quilt teacher, and I've found that my students want to create big, beautiful quilts that look complex but are actually simple to execute. I call these students "time-poor," because they have busy lifestyles but are still eager to make quilts. I developed the designs in this book for people like my students, because *By the Block* concentrates on making quilts using repeats of a single block, simplifying the construction process.

This can be a very effective—and satisfying—way to create. To help those with demanding lives still make dazzling quilts, I've written simple patterns with straightforward instructions, with quick cutting and simple piecing—all requiring no more than basic quilting skills. Rather than relying on a complicated pattern to produce a full-size quilt, the emphasis shifts to careful selection of fabric, concentrating on color and pattern.

Fortunately, finding the perfect fabric to make a stunning quilt is easier today than ever before. Fabric shops are filled with enthusiastic salespeople who are also experienced quilters, and they're eager to share their knowledge when you're browsing. Because complementary lines of fabric are usually in stock, you can quickly find designs that work well together. The Internet has changed the face of crafting in general, and it has had quite an impact on quilting.

If you're not near a good quilting shop, fabric is available 24-7 online, and tutorials become available immediately after a quick search.

Students come into my patchwork classes having taken advantage of what their quilting communities have to offer. Along with friends they've made through quilting, they've taken classes with their favorite designers or watched them on the Internet. They have searched for the perfect fabric (sometimes from their living rooms) and discussed the best piecing techniques with their fellow quilters. Perhaps they've debated about techniques on numerous social media sites. People are far more savvy about what they want and how to get it, and it helps them fit quilting into their full, sometimes hectic days.

Having said all of that, I also get students in my classes who are overwhelmed by all the information and have accumulated a fabric stash

of great proportions but have no idea how to incorporate it into a quilt! *By the Block* is also for those people. They are hungry for ideas and are delighted to have easy-to-execute instructions that tell them how much fabric to purchase, how many squares to cut, and how to piece it all together. Then they can just blissfully sew and at the end have a project they're truly proud of and enjoyed creating. I've taught everyone from young medical students to retired grandmothers, and they all have one thing in common—they want simple quilts that are effective.

By the Block features eighteen quilt patterns based on repeated blocks or units. It's organized by theme, such as the type of block or the construction method, all of which are traditional quilting techniques given a modern twist. Here's an example: One of the best ways to achieve a complex-looking quilt that comes together quickly is to work on a large

scale. You'll see this in quilts such as **Polaroid** (page 124), with its large repeated blocks, or **Churn Dash!** (page 50), which uses just one large block to great advantage. Other designs, such as **Cool Pixels** (page 34) and **Go Big or Go Home** (page 46), feature repetition of smaller blocks; designs like these emphasize fabric choice to make a bold statement.

All the patterns are versatile. Each one lists a finished quilt size and an individual block size, so you can vary the design to fit your needs. I also include general hints with many of the patterns to help save you time and make your quilting a little bit easier. It's just like taking a class with me, minus the distraction of gossip and laughter!

Speaking of me, my true foray into quilting started more than sixteen years ago, when I was as busy as my students are now. I was lucky enough to have a little quilting store nearby,

and I remember buying floral and 1930s reproduction fabrics to create baby quilts for friends. I bought lots of patchwork magazines and quizzed my Nana Sylvia and Aunt Kirsten on how to do everything. (Nana helped me cut out and piece my first quilt tops, which I was inspired to create after receiving a gift of a baby quilt made by Aunt Kirsten.)

I didn't have the time to take a class or join a group with a new baby and a university degree to finish, but I decided that I wanted my children to have handmade things like the ones I had treasured as a child. Despite my full life, I started sporadically making quilts for family and friends in what spare time I had. Now I'm happy to help fellow time-poor quilters continue to have a creative outlet, and I hope the designs in this book—with their emphasis on simplicity of design and ease of construction—will inspire you to do the same.

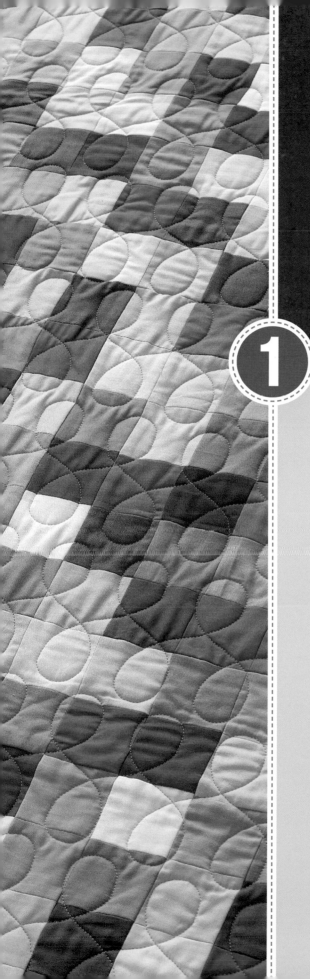

Techniques & Tools

1

If you're familiar with basic quilting techniques, you should be able to make any project in *By the Block*. As a busy quilter, quilt teacher, and mother of four children who are constantly on the go, I have some tips about working efficiently that I'd like to share with you in this chapter. All the patterns that follow (beginning on page 24) were developed to make the creative process as efficient and enjoyable as possible; in fact, only four quilts require templates, and the rest are constructed with easy-to-cut pieces.

◀ *Spontaneous piecing helps this design come together quickly (Cool Pixels, page 34).*

Choosing Fabrics

The quilt patterns in this book are effective because they make clever use of simple pieced blocks, many of which are large in scale, so the construction is quick and easy. But the designs also work because the fabrics used in them are fresh and visually engaging, and the color schemes are intriguing. If you're intimidated by choosing fabrics, it's much like anything else: the more you do it, the better you become at it. In time, you'll feel more confident selecting fabric and choosing colors. Every wonderful quilt starts with the fabrics it's made from.

Color Tips

If you're wary about choosing colors and mixing patterns, I suggest you begin by using a fabric collection—perhaps from a favorite designer—that offers a variety of complementary colors and prints. As you become more comfortable, you can use the color dots on the selvedge as a prompt to help you choose new fabrics that feature the same hues. The dots show the different colors used in the design, so the information from the selvedge can be a great way to educate yourself about color and to learn how to think outside the box about combining patterns.

Pattern and Scale

Prints bring life to many of the designs in this book. I try to match scale of design and hue (color) when I'm choosing fabrics for quilts that require cohesiveness. By scale, I mean the size of the design printed onto the fabric. If I'm combining a floral design with a polka dot, for example, the flowers might be close to the size of the dot. When I'm working on a scrappy look, however, I throw these ideas out the window and try to pay as little attention to hue and scale as possible! Many people find this approach to be very challenging, but again, with time, you'll learn to trust your instincts.

Several of the projects in the book were developed specifically to showcase the beauty of the fabric's design and to demonstrate how important fabric can be to a successful project. In **Go Big or Go Home** (page 46), I had some amazing Marimekko fabric in my stash that featured a large-scale pattern. I had a difficult time finding the right project for it until I realized that the large-scale repeat on the fabric needed to be wed to a simple design that featured large blocks, so the fabric remained the star. Similarly, **Come Flying**

Stripes, plaids, and checks—fabrics that are not always complementary—can work in harmony if paired with a neutral background as in Come Flying (page 74).

Which Fabric is Best?

The vast majority of the quilts in *By the Block* are made from cottons, but I'm a big fan of linen because it's lovely to cut, sews beautifully, and always seems to have a subtle color palette that resonates with me. When selecting a type of fabric, the first question I tend to ask is about the recipient of the quilt. I certainly want to choose sturdy yet comfortable natural fiber if the quilt is for a baby or toddler, as it will likely need to be washed frequently. For pieces that won't require washing so often, the sky is the limit: silks, gauze, even wools can be incorporated into your quilting. Do choose fabrics of similar weights and care requirements to avoid puckering and sagging.

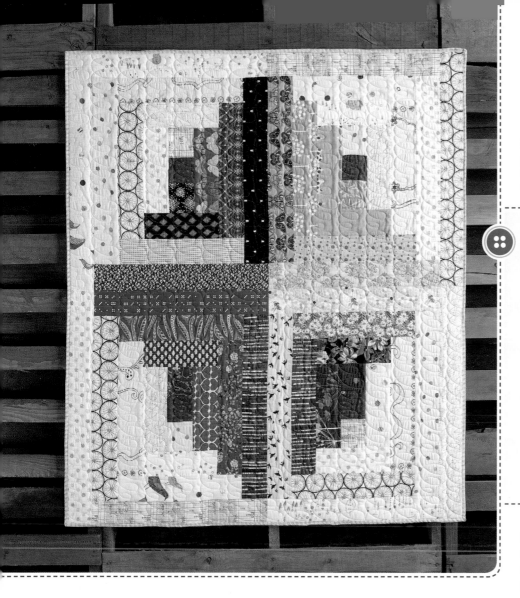

Because of their scale, the lively neutral prints used in this quilt don't distract from the brightly colored fabrics in this variation of Color Burst (page 98).

Be Kind to Your Back

On an ergonomic note, I like to have a fairly high surface for cutting fabric. I find that having to stoop or lean forward is a bit hard on my lower back and neck. No more cutting on the kitchen table for me! I now have a custom cutting surface that is much less stressful on my body. If you don't have an appropriately high cutting table, look for a set of risers meant for lifting a bed off the floor. Slipping them under the legs of your table may yield just the extra height you need.

(page 74) features a lively assortment of checks and plaids—patterns that don't always play nicely with one another! But set against a neutral gray background, the large triangles in the design balance each other.

The concept of balance in pattern and scale is an important one, because it can help unite a collection of fabrics. Many of my ideas about both color and pattern can be seen in one of the variations of the **Color Burst** design, shown above. Note that although all the neutral fabrics are actually busy prints, they relax in the background while the brighter red, blue, yellow, and purple patterns have all the fun.

Preparing Fabric

To wash or not to wash? I'm asked this question often. I neither prewash my quilting fabrics bought by the yard nor launder any high-quality designer fabrics. I find most of them have been preshrunk and made colorfast during the manufacturing process. I also like to work with the fabric while it still has the sizing in it, and unwashed fabric retains its moth protection, which protects it during storage. Long live the fabric stash!

I make a couple of exceptions, however. I do prewash hand-dyed fabric or any fabric that has a reputation for shrinking more than the standard 1 or 2 percent. In those cases, I would prewash, starch, and iron. It's a good idea to apply the same treatment to all the fabrics in a project; either prewash all or none. After construction, I wash my finished quilts in my home machine on a cold wash and add a color catcher to the first wash just to be safe.

Cutting Fabric

I use basic tools for most cutting tasks: a self-healing cutting mat, long gridded acrylic ruler, and rotary cutter. To cut efficiently and safely, always have a sharp blade in your rotary cutter. I generally change the blade on my rotary cutter after each

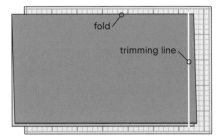

Go Big or Go Home (page 46) features large-scale half-square triangle units that piece together very quickly.

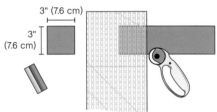

figure 1

figure 2

quilt. A blunt or nicked blade will make cutting a harder job, which can result in sore hands and shoulders; it can also cause mistakes or create uneven edges on the fabric, leading to inaccurate piecing. Of course, make sure you always close your rotary cutter when not in use. They are incredibly sharp, so please be careful.

When I'm working with light slippery fabrics, I like to iron and spray-starch the fabric before I cut; I did this with the Liberty of London Tana Lawn fabrics I used in a couple of projects in the book. If the fabric is extra slippery, I may also use some masking or quilter's tape on the underside of my ruler for a bit of grab, although I'm careful not to cover the grids so I can still cut accurately.

Fabric is generally cut in strips from selvedge to selvedge—you'll see this referred to as WOF (width of fabric) on the project instructions. Cutting in this way gives the cut pieces the most stability. The only time you may cut differently is when you are fussy-cutting a particular piece or trying to maintain the direction of a print, as in **Wild Horses** (page 118). Before you begin to cut, square up your fabric to ensure accurate cuts and straight grain **(FIGURE 1)**.

Crosscutting

Crosscutting is an economical way to cut strips of fabric into smaller units, such as squares. For example, if your pattern calls for a number of 3" (7.5 cm) squares, first cut a 3" (7.5 cm) strip of fabric from selvedge to selvedge, then crosscut the strips into 3" (7.5 cm) squares **(FIGURE 2)**. Layers of strips can be stacked and cut to make the best use of your time; see the Time-saver! at right for more tips about cutting.

time-saver! I'm a fanatic about keeping a sharp blade in my rotary cutter, because it can also save you time. You can stack and cut many layers of fabric simultaneously with a sharp cutter—six to twelve, depending on the size of your rotary blade—reducing repetitive cutting in a quilt with lots of pieces. You can also fold fabric in half lengthwise a second time after squaring to quickly cut strips with your rotary cutter **(FIGURE 3)**, but be very sure the edges are square and the folds are straight to avoid wavy strips.

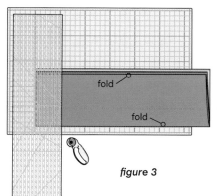

figure 3

 Essential Tool Kit

The individual project instructions will specify any particular tools you may need, but each of the items in this list should be on hand for any quilt you make.

- ○ Quilter's acrylic ruler
- ○ Self-healing cutting mat
- ○ Rotary cutter
- ○ Quilter's flat-head pins
- ○ Sharp seam ripper
- ○ Tape measure
- ○ Embroidery scissors
- ○ Pincushion
- ○ Design wall for quilt layout (a floor will do in a pinch)

Piecing Techniques

The projects in *By the Block* are all created using basic piecing techniques; none are difficult and all are easy to learn if you're not familiar with them. Here are the simple techniques you will use to work faster (and be happier) while you're creating the blocks in each quilt.

Stacking Units

If you're constructing a quilt top with many rows of smaller squares, it's helpful to arrange the squares and then stack them in proper sewing

Take advantage of piecing techniques such as stacking units when working on a quilt with a number of smaller squares.

order (**FIGURES 4 AND 5**). You may find this technique especially useful in a design such as **Love and Be Loved** (page 30), where the quilt's background is composed of many squares.

Chain Piecing

One of the best ways to work quickly is to use chain piecing whenever you can. Chain piecing allows you to stitch pairs of pieces together in a continuous length, saving both time and thread. It begins with organization.

1 Stack the units that you want to join beside your sewing machine, wrong side up, with the edges to be sewn on the right (**FIGURE 6**).

2 Feed the first pair through the machine and then continue with the second pair of pieces (**FIGURE 7**), leaving the units connected by a short chain of thread (**FIGURE 8**). Rows of patches can be assembled into blocks in the same manner, sometimes called chain piecing plus.

Half-Square Triangle Piecing

The half-square triangle (HST) unit—made from two half-square triangles—is one of the most commonly used blocks in quilting. It's easy to create from two equal-sized squares. The HST unit is extremely versatile and can be turned every which way to create intriguing patterns, as you see in **Hoo Are You?** (page 40).

1 Carefully draw a diagonal line on the wrong side of one of the squares from corner to corner; avoid stretching the fabric along the bias as you mark the line.

2 Place the marked square on the second square, right sides facing. Sew the squares together using two seams, ¼" (6 mm) from each side of the marked line (**FIGURE 9**).

3 Cut the squares apart along the line to make two HST units; press each seam open (**FIGURE 10**).

4 Optional: For greatest accuracy, the initial squares may be cut a little larger than necessary. Trim the HST unit to the correct size as given in the instructions for the quilt you're making.

Seams Right

There is a standard seam allowance for quilting—¼" (6 mm). If you've been a garment sewer and are new to quilting, you may default to a ⅝" (1.5 cm) seam allowance without realizing it, but remember that piecing uses much narrower seams. I suggest you use a ¼" (6 mm) quilting foot or mark the ¼" (6 mm) line on your throat plate clearly to ensure the greatest accuracy when piecing.

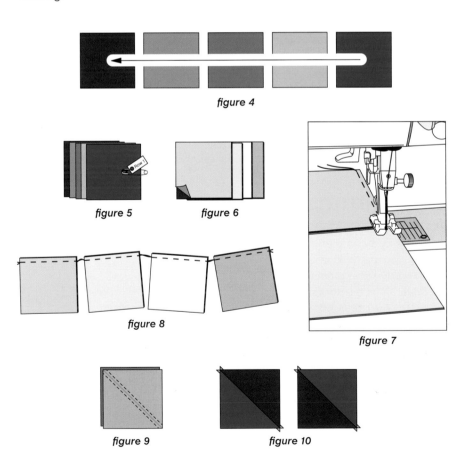

figure 4

figure 5

figure 6

figure 7

figure 8

figure 9

figure 10

Triangle Piecing

If you work on any of the projects in the **Triangle section** (page 72), there are a few things to keep in mind so you can work with these pieces most successfully.

There's a tricky thing about triangles—at least one side is cut on the bias, so it's prone to stretching. It's important to be gentle when you are joining triangles together. It's also helpful to use a straight stitch plate, with a single round hole for the needle rather than a wider slot, to keep the triangle points from being pushed into your sewing machine.

You may also find it helpful to begin sewing on a scrap of fabric, using the chain-piecing technique to continue onto the triangle point. Lastly,

consider using a sturdy fabric such as cotton broadcloth for your first project with triangles.

Log Cabin Piecing

The Log Cabin block is one of the most recognizable in all of quilting, yet it is still used every day in innovative patterns. And it's fun to make! In the **Log Cabin section** (page 92), I use several variations on the traditional block that are outlined in each individual project, but the basics still apply.

1 A Log Cabin block begins with a central square that is surrounded by strips (the "logs"), and the construction sequence is indicated in a block diagram such as the one you see here **(FIGURE 11)**.

2 After each successive strip is added, it's trimmed to match the assembled portion of the block, so strips don't have to be cut to measure before assembly **(FIGURE 12)**. Press the seam allowances away from the center as you work.

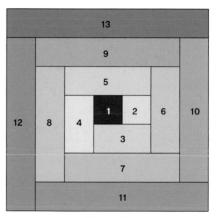

figure 11

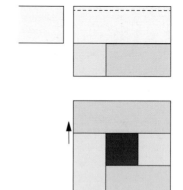

figure 12

Curved piecing can be done very successfully if you use the techniques shown below (FIGURES 13–17).

Curved Piecing

Curved pieces can make an ordinary design extraordinary by softening the geometry of a square or rectangular block. See **Trinity** (page 112) for an example of how a circular element can lend a great deal of mystery to a design. Curved piecing is not difficult. I've found this to be the most successful way to piece these blocks.

1. Mark the center of both the convex and concave pieces by folding each in half and pressing (**FIGURE 13**).

2. Match the centers and use one pin to secure the pieces, right sides together (**FIGURE 14**).

3. Sew the seam in two steps. Begin by aligning one straight edge of each piece (**FIGURE 15**); stitch the seam from that edge to the center pin, easing the pieces to fit (**FIGURE 16**).

4. Repeat from the opposite end of the seam, overlapping the seam ends at the center for a smooth curve (**FIGURE 17**).

Pressing

After you piece, you must press. I work a little differently than most quilters when it comes to seams: I almost *always* press my seams open. This is just my personal preference. I like my quilt tops to lie very flat, and the long-arm machine quilter I use most often (hello, Kim!) has a preference for open seams because it's easier to quilt over flat seams rather than bulky ones. It is also much easier to quilt a project made with a heavier-weight fabric such as denim or upholstery yardage if the seams are pressed open.

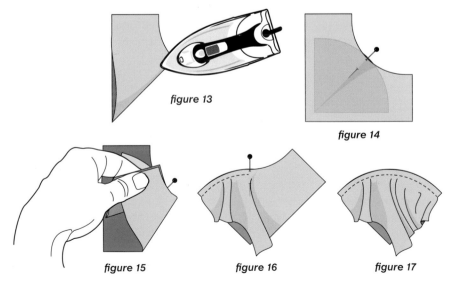

figure 13

figure 14

figure 15

figure 16

figure 17

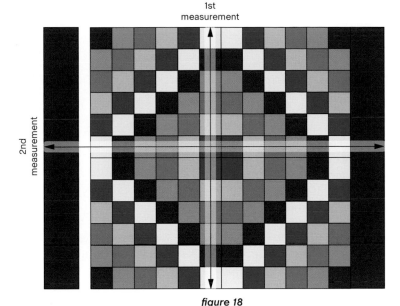

1st measurement

2nd measurement

figure 18

Adding Borders

Through my years of teaching, I've developed a method of adding borders that I feel provides better results than specifying a measurement before the quilt top is constructed. I suggest that my students trim and square their quilt tops and *then* measure to determine the length of the border pieces.

In the patterns I write, I provide the width and number of strips that will be needed to complete the border, but let each quilter assemble his or her own border strips to fit. Here's why: Although all quilters strive to have perfect ¼" (6 mm) seams, it just doesn't always happen. Fabric may stretch, cutting may have been inconsistent, or the measurement on the throat plate or quilting foot may be slightly off. Using this method, my students don't cut a border to a specified measurement only to discover it is ½" (1.3 cm) too short!

1 Trim the assembled quilt, squaring the corners as necessary.

2 Measure the assembled quilt top through the center (**FIGURE 18**). The center of the quilt is less likely to be distorted than the edges, providing a truer measurement. Assemble the first border strips and trim to make two borders matching the measurement.

3 Add the first two border pieces (either the side or top and bottom borders) to the quilt top. As you sew on the border strips, distribute any extra fullness along the entire length of the seam and ease it into place. Press the seam allowances toward the border strips.

4 Measure through the center of the quilt, including the newly added border pieces, and cut the remaining border strips to match that

length; sew them to the quilt top and press the seam allowances toward the borders.

I have another tip or two about constructing borders. When seaming is necessary to make a border long enough to fit your quilt, try to position the seam about a third of the way down the border's length; the eye is not drawn to it in this spot. Also try to make sure that the seams are not directly opposite one another; this can draw too much attention to them, distracting the eye from your lovely quilt top. When you have sufficient fabric, use diagonal seams to piece the border strips, further disguising the seams.

Your Machine at the Ready

All sewing machines are different, especially with all the whiz-bang features some offer, but most generally have similar attachments. I live by my ¼" (6 mm) foot and straight stitch plate, and I recommend these accessories for piecing quilts. A sharp needle is a must; as a general rule you should change the needle on your machine after each quilt. You may be surprised at the difference this simple step can make in the symmetry of your stitches. I also highly recommend yearly maintenance for your machine; they accumulate a lot of lint and need some TLC to keep all their parts moving smoothly.

Finishing Your Quilt

After the piecing is done, you must turn your beautiful quilt top into a finished quilt. All of the projects in *By the Block* use these easy, simple finishing techniques: making a backing, adding the batting, joining all the layers together by quilting, and binding the edges. Feel free to use your favorite techniques to finish your quilt, but here are some thoughts on the process.

Backing

Generally speaking, a simple quilt backing can be made from a long piece of yardage that is cut in two and stitched together lengthwise after its selvedges are removed; you'll see requirements for a backing of this type in each set of project instructions. I prefer to make pieced backings for my quilts, often using leftovers from the quilt top, but this is not necessary unless you

welcome the extra creativity. If you're looking for some quick ways to piece your backing decoratively, try one of these ideas: join four large rectangles **(FIGURE 19)**; add a horizontal strip for a pop of color **(FIGURE 20)**; or dive into your stash and use a combination of fat quarters **(FIGURE 21)**.

Another preference of mine is to add a generous amount of extra fabric to the backing. The patterns in this book include enough fabric for an 8" (20.5 cm) fabric margin in each dimension of the backing, or 4" (10 cm) on each side. That amount provides extra fabric for handling and quilting the quilt sandwich, while minimizing the total amount of fabric required.

My personal choice is to allow 6" to 7" (15 to 18 cm) on each side, or 12" to 14" (30.5 to 35.5 cm) overall, when piecing my backings. If your project is heavily quilted, you may need the extra fabric, and I would advise you to be safe rather than

time-saver! Because you must always press your seams before the next units can be added to your quilt top, I find it helps to set up the iron right next to my sewing machine. You can lose a lot of time going back and forth to your ironing board.

sorry. Remember to purchase extra fabric if you plan to cut your backing larger than is suggested in the project instructions, or extend the size by creating a pieced backing as described in this section. If you work with a long-arm quilter, ask about her preferences before cutting your backing to size.

Also note that the seam(s) in the backing may run horizontally or vertically. Sometimes that's the difference between needing two or three quilt-lengths of fabric.

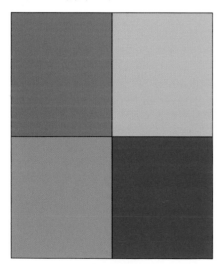

figure 19

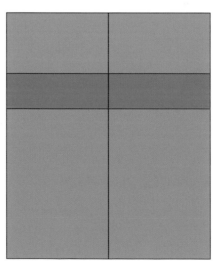

figure 20

figure 21

If you have leftover strips after piecing your quilt top, you can use them to create a striking backing.

needs to be prewashed before use. On the other hand, shrinkage may work to your advantage if you want that really lofty look and feel.

Speaking of loft, this quality is also important; low-loft battings are thin, while high-loft battings are thick and fluffy. Like backing, batting should be cut larger than the quilt top all the way around, usually the same size as the backing fabric or 1" (2.5 cm) smaller on each side (6" to 8" [15 to 20.5 cm] larger than the quilt top overall).

Basting

Basting is the method used to secure the quilt top to the backing and batting in preparation for quilting. There are several ways you can do this, and I encourage you to use your favorite technique. The quilt sandwich, as it is called, can be secured with hand basting, large safety pins, or even adhesive basting spray.

Press the quilt top before you assemble the quilt sandwich and work from the center out as you baste the layers. All the quilts in *By the Block* are finished with binding, so they are all stacked in the same way: backing, right side down; batting in the middle; and quilt top, right side up. Center the batting and quilt top over the backing.

Batting

My usual go-to batting is low-loft wool that has been needle punched. It's lightweight, breathable, and doesn't shift or migrate after numerous washes. The quilting distance—the maximum distance between lines of stitching—is 2" to 3" (5 to 7.5 cm), depending on the manufacturer. There is a vast array of batting available, including products made from cotton, polyester, bamboo, and blends. If you live in a warmer climate, a cotton batting may be more comfortable in your quilts; if you're striving for economy, consider a polyester-cotton blend from a reputable manufacturer for a good combination of texture and price.

There are a few things to keep in mind while you're shopping for batting. Batting can shrink significantly, depending on the fiber content and batting construction, so investigate whether the batting you choose

The quilting pattern used on Trinity (page 112) helps reinforce the circular theme of the design.

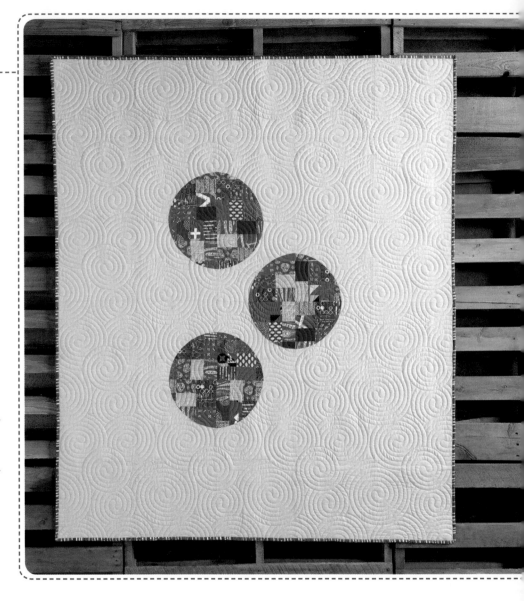

Quilting

Although any project can be quilted on a home machine, you will also see that many of the quilts in this book have been quilted on a long-arm machine. Originally I used a professional, because I was nervous about quilting my own large quilts—I was very confident in piecing king-size quilts but not so confident in quilting them. Now, after creating many, many quilts, confidence is not the problem—it's time, as you may have guessed.

Honestly, I'm very satisfied with the variety of the overall pantograph patterns available for a long-arm machine. A professional long-arm quilter can also create a custom design that complements the design of the quilt top, and often this is the final decorative touch that makes a quilt spectacular. On the practical side, a quilt that has been finished on a long-arm machine is extremely sturdy and can be washed often without showing signs of wear.

Not everyone is able to use a professional long-arm quilter, due to availability or economics. Please don't underestimate the importance of the quilting to the overall success of your project, because it can affect the aesthetics of the quilt top you've worked so hard to complete. I often ask my students to think about how a project will be quilted before they even pick a pattern or select fabric.

When I quilt my own designs, I often use simple straight-line quilting or a variation called echo quilting to finish off my quilts. Echo quilting follows the shape of the design in your quilt; see the detail from **Lullaby** on page 21 for an example. When you're quilting on your home machine, I suggest adjusting the stitch length to a setting between 3.5 and 4.5, depending on the amount of bulk in the quilt; the bulkier quilt will feed through the machine more slowly, making the stitches appear shorter. Stitch at a slow pace; for more consistent stitches, reduce your machine's speed setting if you can. See the sidebar on the next page for information about accessories for home quilting.

Echo quilting is a good choice for the quilter who wants to finish quilts on a domestic sewing machine.

It's All About the Feet

If you will be doing your own quilting, several accessories for your machine will be quite helpful. First is a walking foot, also called an even-feed foot. This great gadget moves the upper layers of fabric through your machine while the feed dogs handle the lower layers, so your quilt sandwich is fed through at a consistent rate.

If you're interesting in free-motion stitching, you'll need a specialty foot also—a darning foot. Find one with an open toe for the best visibility as you stitch.

Free-motion quilting is another popular way to finish a quilt; this is basically drawing with your needle. Once perfected, free-motion quilting can give you great design freedom in finishing your quilts. Invest some time in learning free-motion quilting if you're interested in this nifty technique. The common forms of free-motion quilting include stippling, loops, meandering lines, and figure eights, but really any design is within your reach. Different machines require specific settings for free-motion quilting. Generally, it involves lowering or covering the feed dogs, but be sure to check the instructions on your particular machine for specifics.

Binding

The majority of my quilts have easy machine-sewn binding. Truthfully, this is my impatience showing, because I'm not someone who enjoys the hand-binding process. I wish I were patient, because other people look like they're having fun relaxing and watching TV while they're binding. I also find that a machine-sewn binding stands up to frequent washing well, which is especially important for

kids' quilts. This is really important to me, because I have four kids!

While my general advice is to finish the binding by hand when you can—it's a neater finish—don't stress if it's not your thing or if time is an issue (our recurring theme once again). It's a very quick process to make a binding, whether you stitch by hand or by machine. You'll begin with the number of strips specified in the project instructions.

1 After quilting, trim the backing and batting even with the quilt top and make sure the corners are square.

2 Remove the selvedges and stitch all the strips together into one long piece of binding, right sides together. I prefer to use straight joins, but you may substitute diagonal seams to reduce bulk in the folded binding. Trim the seam allowances to ¼" (6 mm), if necessary, and press the seams open **(FIGURE 22)**. Fold the binding strip in half lengthwise, wrong sides together, and press.

3 Begin applying the binding near one corner of the quilt. Lay the prepared binding strip on the quilt top, matching the raw edges, and leaving 8" to 10" (20.5 to 25.5 cm) of the binding free for finishing **(FIGURE 23)**. Backstitch and sew the binding to the quilt with a ¼" (6 mm) seam allowance.

4 When you reach the corner, stop stitching ¼" (6 mm) from the quilt edge **(FIGURE 24)**. Backstitch to secure the line of stitching. Rotate the quilt into position to stitch the next side and fold the binding up at a 45-degree angle to create a mitered corner. Now fold the binding down to align with the next side of the quilt and stitch the second side **(FIGURE 25)**, again stopping ¼" (6 mm) from the corner. Repeat around the quilt.

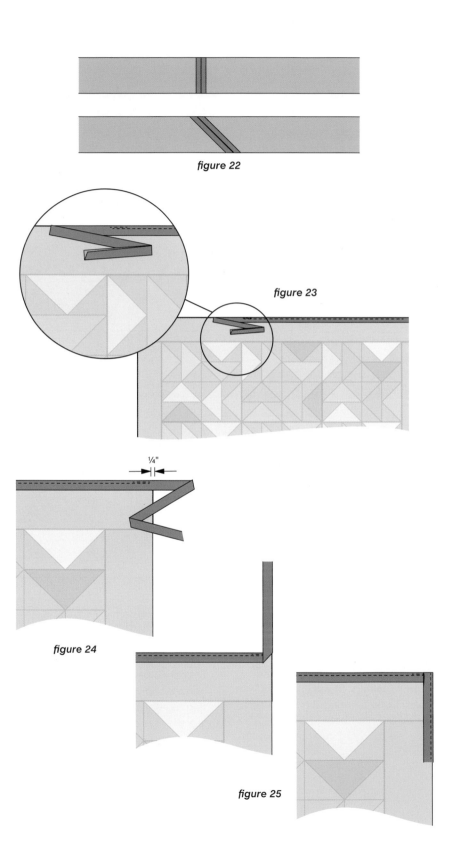

figure 22

figure 23

figure 24

figure 25

Add visual interest to a standard binding with triangle inserts; read about this technique on page 77.

time-saver! Want to build a quick binding? Use jelly roll strips instead of cutting your own strips. Every quilt in this book calls for 2½" (6.5 cm) binding strips, the same width as a jelly roll strip.

Not Just for Zippers Anymore

I've recently discovered a great trick I'd like to share with you: I use my zipper foot to stitch binding onto my quilts. It holds the binding in place securely, and I can consistently stay on the edge of the binding when I'm sewing. Try it!

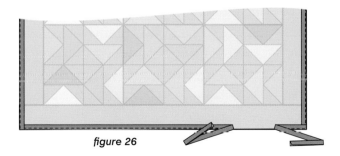

figure 26

5 When you near the starting point, stop sewing and secure the seam with backstitches **(FIGURE 26)**. Smooth the beginning tail of the binding into place along the edge of the quilt and arrange the end of the binding strip to overlap it. Trim the excess binding, leaving a ½" (1.3 cm) overlap for seam allowances.

6 Unfold the loose ends of the binding, position the two ends of the binding with right sides together, and stitch. Press the seam allowances open. Refold and press the binding, then sew the remainder of the binding strip to the quilt.

7 Fold the binding to the back of the quilt over the raw edges, just covering the seam line; shape the miters at the corners and pin into place. Stitch the binding to the back by hand with a slip stitch or by machine, working from the back of the quilt. At right, see my tip for finishing binding with your machine.

Squares

2

Want to get started building quilts based on a repeated block? Begin here. The projects in this section are based on simple squares and don't have complicated instructions, but each of them demonstrates how important your fabric choices are when you're working with basic repeats of a single block. Quick piecing techniques help you enjoy every minute you spend on one of these quilts.

◄ *Detail from Love and Be Loved, page 30*

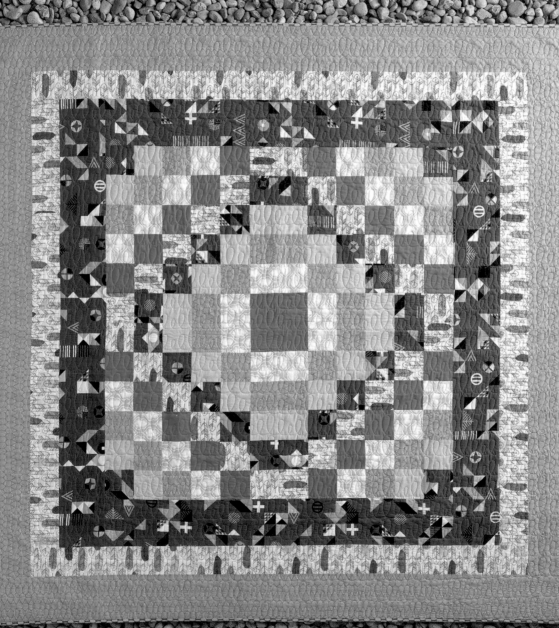

BLOCK SIZE: 24" × 24" (61 × 61 cm)

QUILT SIZE: 76" × 76" (193 × 193 cm)

PIECED BY Siobhan Rogers

LONG-ARM QUILTED BY Kim Bradley

Trip Around My World

materials

All fabric amounts are for 45" (114.5 cm) wide fabric unless otherwise noted

1½ yd (1.4 m) red print fabric

1⅞ yd (1.7 m) teal print fabric

⅝ yd (57 cm) teal solid fabric

⅝ yd (57 cm) yellow text print fabric

⅝ yd (57 cm) yellow print fabric

1¼ yd (1.1 m) white print fabric

4¾ yd (4.4 m) backing fabric

⅔ yd (61 cm) binding fabric

84" × 84" (213.5 × 213.5 cm) batting

tools

Essential tool kit (page 13)

Sometimes quilt designs are an accumulation of events and ideas all rolled into one.

I had been experimenting with the traditional Trip Around the World pattern and wanted to play more with color, direction, and size. That same morning I was eating a ruby red grapefruit on a turquoise plate . . . seeing the juxtaposition of the red fruit, yellow skin, white pith, and turquoise plate gave me just the color palette I was looking for.

cut the fabric

WOF = width of fabric

From red print fabric:

- cut 4 strips 4¼" (11 cm) × WOF
- cut 5 strips 6½" (16.5 cm) × WOF

From teal print fabric:

- cut 4 strips 4¼" (11 cm) × WOF
- cut 7 strips 6½" (16.5 cm) × WOF

From teal solid fabric, cut 4 strips 4¼" (11 cm) × WOF

From yellow text print fabric, cut 4 strips 4¼" (11 cm) × WOF

From yellow print fabric, cut 4 strips 4¼" (11 cm) × WOF

From white print fabric:

- cut 4 strips 4¼" (11 cm) × WOF
- cut 6 strips 4¼" (11 cm) × WOF

From binding fabric, cut 8 strips 2½" (6.5 cm) × WOF

From backing fabric, cut 2 rectangles 84" (213.5 cm) × WOF

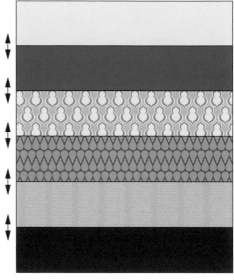

figure 1

Make the Block

1 Piece one 4¼" (11 cm) strip from each of the six fabrics together in the following order: white print, teal solid, yellow print, teal print, yellow text print, red print **(FIGURE 1)**. Press the seams open. Repeat to make four identical strip sets.

2 Fold one strip set lengthwise with right sides together and stitch, forming a tube. Press the seam open. Repeat for the remaining three strip sets.

3 Crosscut each tube into 4¼" (11 cm) strips **(FIGURE 2)**. You will use twenty-four strips in the quilt; save the remaining pieced fabric or strips to add to your backing if desired.

4 Separate the pieced strips into four groups of six. Working with one group at a time, unpick a different seam in each strip, beginning

with the seam between the white print and the red print. Remove the seam in each remaining strip in sequence, working around the loop. Organize the open strips as shown in the **BLOCK DIAGRAM** (see page 29) and stitch together, pressing the seams open. Repeat with the remaining strip groups to make four identical blocks.

Make the Quilt Top

5 Refer to the **CONSTRUCTION DIAGRAM** and arrange the blocks so the solid teal squares meet at the center (see page 29). Stitch the blocks together, pressing the seams open.

6 Trim the quilt top so the corners are square and the sides are straight. Measure the dimensions of the trimmed quilt top in preparation for assembling the borders.

4¼" (11 cm)

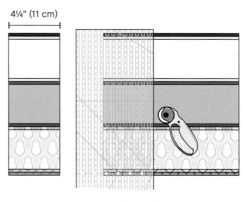

figure 2

7 Add a red print border from the 6½" (16.5 cm) strips, a white print border from the remaining 4¼" (11 cm) strips, and a teal print border from the 6½" (16.5 cm) strips. Refer to my method of measuring and assembling the borders in sequence on page 17.

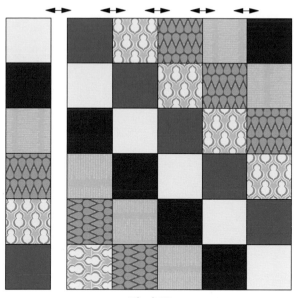

Block Diagram

Finish the Quilt

8 Make a backing as desired, referring to Finishing Your Quilt (page 18) as needed. Feel free to use your favorite methods for the finishing steps, including constructing a pieced backing if you would like.

9 Make a quilt sandwich from the backing, batting, and quilt top. Baste all layers together.

10 Quilt as desired, then trim the backing and batting to match the quilt top.

11 Join the binding strips to form a continuous length. Bind the raw edges to finish the quilt.

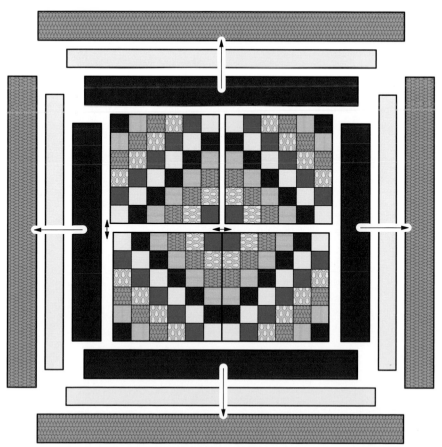

Construction Diagram

✱ **tip**

In the construction of this quilt top, the block units are rotated, changing the orientation of the prints; notice the white print in the central blocks. When you're choosing fabrics for this quilt, pay attention to the direction of the prints you're considering and decide whether you need to adjust the piecing steps to allow for your print—or not!

BLOCK SIZE: Varies

QUILT SIZE: 63" × 78" (160 × 198 cm)

PIECED BY Siobhan Rogers

LONG-ARM QUILTED BY Kim Bradley

Love and Be Loved

materials

*All fabric amounts are for 45"
(114.5 cm) wide fabric unless
otherwise noted*

17 fat quarters (18" × 22"
[45.5 × 56 cm]) in various prints

1¼ yd (1.1 m) brown polka-dot fabric

4 yd (3.7 m) backing fabric

⅔ yd (61 cm) binding fabric

72" × 87" (183 × 221 cm) batting

tools

Essential tool kit (page 13)

A quilt is a lovely reminder of love. This quilt is in
remembrance of my parents and all the support they
gave me as I grew up, and the words on the quilt
were inspired by a BBC production about lost love,
Birdsong. The letters in the heartfelt message are built
rather simply with a combination of squares and half-
square triangle units (HSTs) in a brown polka-dot linen
fabric that is a nice contrast to the Liberty of London
Tana Lawn fat quarters. Though some of the letters
are formed with HSTs, most of the quilt is composed
of basic squares.

You can incorporate an additional message into the backing of your quilt if you desire.

cut the fabric

WOF = width of fabric

From fat quarters:

○ cut a total of 404 squares 3½" × 3½" (9 × 9 cm)

○ cut a total of 20 squares 4" × 4" (10 × 10 cm)

From brown polka-dot fabric:

○ cut 10 strips 3½" (9 cm) × WOF; crosscut into 102 squares 3½" × 3½" (9 × 9 cm)

○ cut 2 strips 4" (10 cm) × WOF; crosscut into 20 squares 4" × 4" (10 × 10 cm)

From binding fabric, cut 8 strips 2½" (6.5 cm) × WOF

From backing fabric, cut 2 rectangles 72" (183 cm) × WOF

fyi

Although the Liberty of London fat quarters are 18" × 26½" (45.5 × 67.5 cm), the fabric requirements listed here are based on the standard-size fat quarter. If you use Liberty of London fat quarters, you'll have some beautiful remnants for another project.

Make the Block

1 Make forty half-square triangle units (HSTs, page 14) from the brown and fat quarter fabrics (**FIGURE 1**).

2 Refer to the **BLOCK DIAGRAM** and the **CONSTRUCTION DIAGRAM** to make the letter unit blocks. Each block is a three-square by six-square unit except the ampersand, which is five squares by six squares.

Make the Quilt Top

3 The entire quilt top is composed of twenty-six rows of twenty-one squares each, including the letter units. Refer to the **CONSTRUCTION DIAGRAM** to arrange the units into rows for each letter or symbol. Assemble the rows to complete eachblock.

4 Arrange the letter units on a design wall or other flat surface and position the remaining print squares as in the **CONSTRUCTION DIAGRAM** (see page 33). Stitch the squares between letters into vertical rows. Sew the rows to the letter units, matching seams. Press all seams open. Add horizontal sashing units, two squares high and twenty-one squares wide, to join the letter rows.

NOTE: *Because I wanted to construct the quilt top one square at a time to achieve greatest variety in the fabric arrangement, I did not chain piece (page 14), yet the quilt top came together very quickly. However, you can chain piece while constructing the rows of print squares if you would like to work even more rapidly.*

figure 1

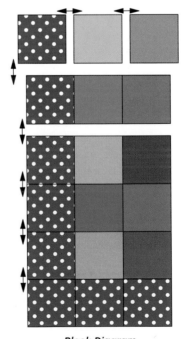

Block Diagram

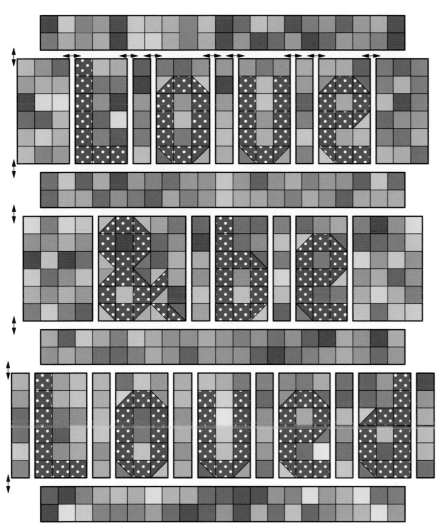

Construction Diagram

Finish the Quilt

5 Make a backing as desired, referring to Finishing Your Quilt (page 18) as needed. Use your favorite methods for the finishing steps if you prefer, including constructing a pieced backing.

6 Make a quilt sandwich from the backing, batting, and quilt top. Baste all layers together.

7 Quilt as desired, then trim the backing and batting to match the quilt top.

8 Join the binding strips to form a continuous length. Bind the raw edges to finish the quilt.

✳ tip

If you would like to construct your own message quilt, you can use the letters in this project as examples to show you how to construct any individual letter. During my design process, I laid out the letters first and then constructed the words. I finished by putting the word blocks on my design wall to determine how to fill in the design with background rows of squares.

BLOCK SIZE: 12" × 12" (30.5 × 30.5 cm)

QUILT SIZE: 60" × 80" (152.5 × 203 cm)

PIECED BY Siobhan Rogers

LONG-ARM QUILTED BY Kim Bradley

Cool Pixels

When I was planning this quilt for a boy's second birthday, I noticed a lot of pixel art as well as a lot of quilts using 2½" (6.5 cm) squares, so the two ideas seemed like a perfect match. I wanted the quilt to be "cool enough" to have on his bed as Mr. Nearly Two grew older, so I picked a pile of bright colors and added three monotone gray blocks to create a focal point. Chain piecing makes the construction of this quilt relatively quick, and it will go even faster if you don't get hung up on the color selection when you're working—be random.

materials

All fabric amounts are for 45" (114.5 cm) wide fabric unless otherwise noted

20 fat quarters (18" × 22" [45.5 × 56 cm]) in various colors

½ yd (45.5 cm) each of 4 different shades of gray fabric, plus an additional ¼ yd (23 cm) in one of the shades

½ yd (45.5 cm) white fabric

¼ yd (23 cm) blue fabric

5 yd (4.6 m) backing fabric

½ yd (45.5 cm) binding fabric

68" × 88" (173 × 223.5 cm) batting

tools

Essential tool kit (page 13)

cut the fabric

WOF = width of fabric

From each fat quarter, cut 42 squares 2½" × 2½" (6.5 × 6.5 cm)

From each gray fabric, cut 60 squares 2½" × 2½" (6.5 × 6.5 cm); from largest gray fabric, also cut 1 strip 8" × 17" (20.5 × 43 cm)

From white fabric, cut 60 squares 2½" × 2½" (6.5 × 6.5 cm)

From blue fabric, cut 1 strip 8" × 44" (20.5 × 112 cm)

From binding fabric, cut 7 strips 2½" (6.5 cm) × WOF

From backing fabric, cut 2 rectangles 88" (223.5 cm) × WOF

fyi

You'll have extra 2½" (6.5 cm) squares to use in the quilt backing or save in your stash. The extras will allow more flexibility as you randomize color placement in the quilt blocks. If you want to replicate my color scheme, here's the formula: I used nine shades of blue, five shades of green, three shades of red, two shades of orange, and one shade of yellow. Finally, I originally planned to appliqué Mr. Nearly Two's name onto the fabric border at the top of the quilt. I ultimately decided I liked it blank, but if you would like to personalize your quilt, the design allows for it.

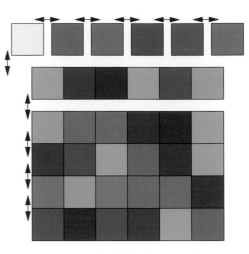

Block Diagram

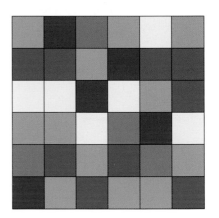

figure 1

Make the Blocks

1 Chain piece six rows of six squares each, arranging the colors randomly. Press the seams open and then join the rows to make a block (see the **BLOCK DIAGRAM** at right). Make a total of thirty blocks, including three that are composed of only gray and white squares **(FIGURE 1)**. Press all of the seams open.

Make the Quilt Top

2 Refer to the **CONSTRUCTION DIAGRAM** (page 37) to stitch the blocks together in rows, pressing the seams open. Stitch the rows together, matching seams. Press the seams open.

3 To make the border, stitch the blue and gray strips together end to end and press the seam open. Stitch the border to the top of the quilt and press the seam open.

Finish the Quilt

4 Make a backing as desired, referring to Finishing Your Quilt (page 18) as needed. Feel free to use your favorite methods for the finishing steps and construct a pieced backing if you'd like—remember that you've got extra squares already cut.

5 Make a quilt sandwich from the backing, batting, and quilt top. Baste all layers together.

6 Quilt as desired, then trim the backing and batting to match the quilt top.

7 Join the binding strips to form a continuous length. Bind the raw edges to finish the quilt.

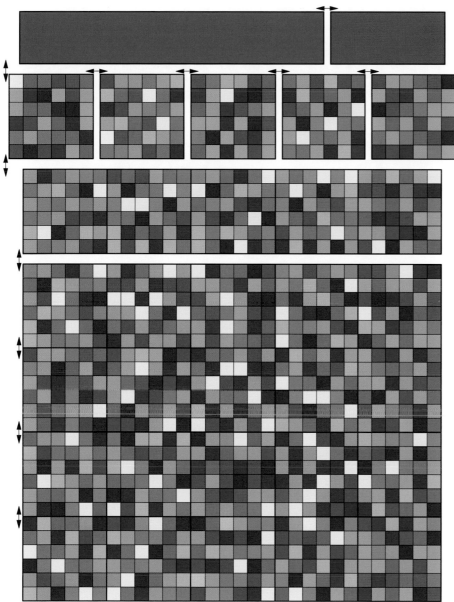

Construction Diagram

time-saver! No time for cutting? Use mini charm packs (precut 2½" [6.5 cm] squares) instead of fat quarters.

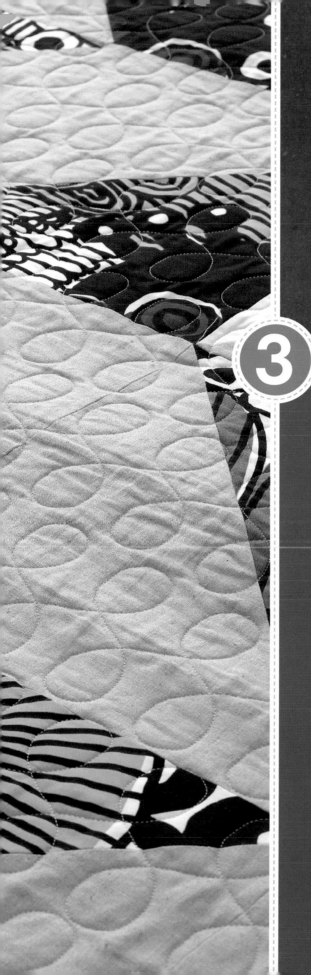

Half–Square Triangles

3

The half-square triangle (HST) is a surprisingly versatile building block, as you'll see in this section. The patterns using this basic unit include quilts based on small HSTs, large HSTs, and one with supersized HSTs that really packs a punch. Explore the possibilities of the traditional half-square triangle in this array of clever quilt designs.

◄ *Large half-square triangle units from Go Big or Go Home, page 46*

BLOCK SIZE: 2½" × 2½" (6.5 × 6.5 cm)

QUILT SIZE: 80" × 85" (203 × 216 cm)

PIECED BY Siobhan Rogers

LONG-ARM QUILTED BY Kim Bradley

LITTLE OWLS FABRIC PANEL BY Kristen Doran

Hoo Are You?

Half-square triangles (HSTs) are so versatile, you can do a million great things with them! I started making this quilt as an example for my students. It's made entirely from HST units, and the patterns in the quilt top are formed by simply changing their orientation. Kristen Doran's adorable owls were the perfect focal points for the central units.

materials

All fabric amounts are for 45" (114.5 cm) wide fabric unless otherwise noted

½ yd (45.5 cm) dark blue chambray fabric

1¾ yd (1.6 m) teal fabric

¾ yd (68.5 cm) pink linen fabric

¾ yd (68.5 cm) orange linen fabric

1 yd (91.5 cm) light blue chambray fabric

1¼ yd (1.2 m) off-white text print fabric

3½ yd (3.2 m) white text print fabric

1 yd (91.5 cm) natural linen fabric

4 focal panels, each cut to 5½" × 8" (14 × 20.5 cm)

7½ yd (6.9 m) backing fabric

88" × 93" (223.5 × 236 cm) batting

NOTE: *When choosing and/or fussy cutting your focal panels, remember that you'll need to allow ¼" (6 mm) seam allowance on each edge, so the designs should measure 5" × 7½" (12.5 x 19 cm) or less.*

tools

Essential tool kit (page 13)

cut the fabric

WOF = width of fabric

From dark blue chambray fabric, cut 6 strips 3½" (9 cm) × WOF; crosscut into 65 squares 3½" × 3½" (9 × 9 cm)

From teal fabric, cut 17 strips 3½" (9 cm) × WOF; crosscut into 184 squares 3½" × 3½" (9 × 9 cm)

From pink linen fabric, cut 7 strips 3½" (9 cm) × WOF; crosscut into 76 squares 3½" × 3½" (9 × 9 cm)

From orange linen fabric, cut 9 strips 3½" (9 cm) × WOF; crosscut into 92 squares 3½" × 3½" (9 × 9 cm)

From light blue chambray fabric, cut 10 strips 3½" (9 cm) × WOF; crosscut into 109 squares 3½" × 3½" (9 × 9 cm)

From the white text print fabric:

○ cut 28 strips 3½" (9 cm) × WOF; crosscut into 300 squares 3½" × 3½" (9 × 9 cm)

○ cut 9 strips 2½" (6.5 cm) × WOF

From the off-white text print fabric, cut 12 strips 3½" (9 cm) × WOF; crosscut into 132 squares 3½" × 3½" (9 × 9 cm)

From the natural linen fabric, cut 10 strips 3½" (9 cm) × WOF; crosscut into 106 squares 3½" × 3½" (9 × 9 cm)

From backing fabric, cut 2 rectangles 88" (223.5 cm) × WOF

fyi

If you prefer to use fat quarters, you'll be able to get thirty squares, each 3½" × 3½" (9 × 9 cm), from each standard fat quarter. If you prefer to use only half-square triangle units (HSTs) throughout, you can replace each owl focal panel with six HST units.

Make the Blocks

1 Following the instructions on page 14, make HST units in the following quantities and color combinations:

Dark blue chambray and off-white text	130
Light blue chambray and off-white text	14
Teal blue and white text	140
Teal blue and off-white text	120
Teal blue and natural linen	108
Pink linen and white text	152
Orange linen and white text	184
Light blue chambray and white text	100
Light blue chambray and natural linen	104
White text and white text	12

Trim each HST unit to measure 3" × 3" (7.5 × 7.5 cm).

2 Arrange a focal panel and thirty-six dark-blue/off-white text HST units to make a block for the central section of the quilt (**FIGURE 1**). Assemble the HSTs above and below the focal panel in rows, then join the rows to make the top and bottom units. Sew the HSTs along the sides of the focal panel together in columns and join the columns to make the side sections. Sew a side section to each side of the focal panel, then add the top and bottom units. Make three additional central units, referring to the Block Diagram for the correct orientation of the HSTs in each section. For a touch of whimsy, substitute fourteen light blue chambray/off-white text HSTs in the upper right central unit. Match all seams and press them open after joining.

3 Sew the four central units together as shown in the **BLOCK DIAGRAM**.

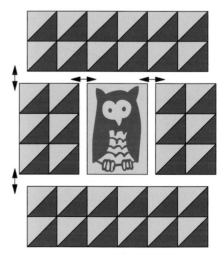

figure 1

Make the Quilt Top

NOTE: *Although you may not be able to tell from the photo on page 40, the corners of the quilt are actually HSTs assembled from two squares of the same white text fabric.*

4 Referring to the **CONSTRUCTION DIAGRAM** on page 44, arrange the remaining HSTs to make two top/bottom sections, two side sections, and four corner sections. Sew the HSTs within each section together in rows, then join the rows to complete the section. Match the seams and press the seam allowances open as you go.

5 Sew a side section to each side of the center section, orienting the sections as shown. Sew a corner section to each end of each top/bottom section, rotating the sections as necessary. Stitch the assembled sections to the top and bottom of the center assembly to complete the quilt top.

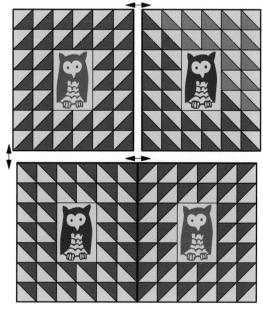

Block Diagram

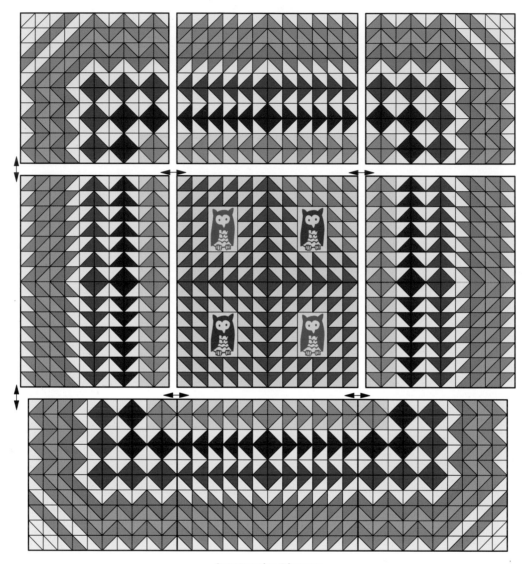

Construction Diagram

Finish the Quilt

6 Make a backing as desired, referring to Finishing Your Quilt (page 18) as needed. Use your favorite methods for the finishing steps if you'd prefer, including constructing a pieced backing.

7 Make a quilt sandwich from the backing, batting, and quilt top. Baste all layers together.

8 Quilt as desired, then trim the backing and batting to match the quilt top.

9 Join the 2½" (6.5 cm) white text binding strips to form a continuous length. Bind the raw edges to finish the quilt.

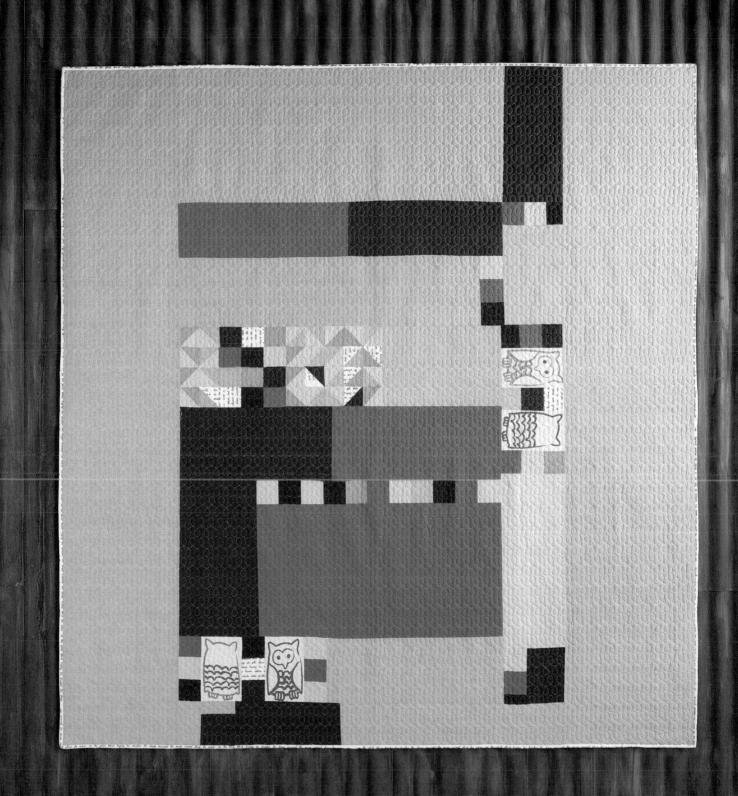

BLOCK SIZE: 12½" × 12½" (31.5 × 31.5 cm)

QUILT SIZE: 87½" × 87½" (222 × 222 cm)

PIECED BY Siobhan Rogers

LONG-ARM QUILTED BY Kim Bradley

Go Big or Go Home

materials

All fabric amounts are for 45" (114.5 cm) wide fabric unless otherwise noted

3¼ yd (3 m) print fabric with a large-scale design

3¼ yd (3 m) blue fabric

8 yd (7.4 m) backing fabric

¾ yd (68.5 cm) binding fabric

96" × 96" (244 × 244 cm) batting

NOTE: *Just for fun, cut one or more binding strips from a contrasting fabric. The contrasting strips do not need to be a full fabric width, but they should be cut 2½" (6.5 cm) wide.*

tools

Essential tool kit (page 13)

I have been buying and collecting fabric since . . . forever. I often have no intentions to use it or know what project it will suit—I just like it and buy it. This Marimekko fabric was one of those buys—I had no idea what to do with it, and I wasn't sure about cutting it up. So it sat in my fabric pile for a few years until I decided to be brave and cut it up. Because it's such a large-scale pattern, I knew the fabric had to be used in large pieces and the quilt top needed to be a simple repeat, so the colors and shapes of the fabulous fabric design wouldn't be lost.

Make the Block

1 You will make large half-square triangle (HSTs) units for this quilt; the method is the same as that for small HSTs, but the results are large scale. Follow the instructions on page 14 to make fifty HSTs from the print and blue fabric as in the **BLOCK DIAGRAM** (see right). Press the seams open. You will use forty-nine blocks; save the remainder for the back of the quilt or another project.

Make the Quilt Top

2 Arrange the HST units in rows, rotating every other block **(FIGURE 1)**. Stitch each row together and press the seams open. The rows are identical; changing the orientation of every other row creates the overall design of the quilt.

Block Diagram

figure 1

Construction Diagram

3 Lay out the rows as shown in the **CONSTRUCTION DIAGRAM** (see above). Stitch the rows together, pressing the seams open.

Finish the Quilt

4 Make a backing as desired, referring to Finishing Your Quilt (page 18) as needed. You'll need to cut and assemble three fabric lengths to create the necessary width, or you can begin with two fabric lengths and add pieces left over from other projects to expand the backing sufficiently. Feel free to use your favorite methods for the finishing steps.

5 Make a quilt sandwich from the backing, batting, and quilt top. Baste all layers together.

6 Quilt as desired, then trim the backing and batting to match the quilt top.

7 Join the binding strips to form a continuous length. Bind the raw edges to finish the quilt.

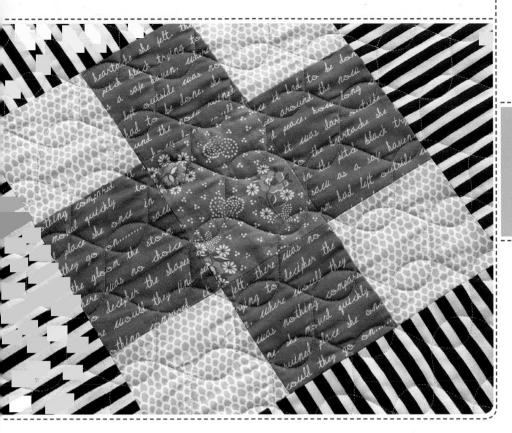

BLOCK SIZE: Varies

QUILT SIZE: 48" × 49" (122 × 124.5 cm)

PIECED BY Siobhan Rogers

LONG-ARM QUILTED BY Kim Bradley

Churn Dash!

When I visited the American Folk Art Museum, I started thinking about where quilting came from and how it developed. This supersized interpretation of the traditional churn dash motif—just one single block made with simple piecing—was inspired by that visit. The quilt is big enough for a crib or throw quilt, but the design can be easily adapted: two blocks with a larger sashing on the sides would make a lovely single bed quilt (especially if the block was put on the diagonal) and four blocks would make a great king-size quilt.

materials

All fabric amounts are for 45" (114.5 cm) wide fabric unless otherwise noted

4½" × 5½" (11.5 × 14 cm) rectangle of pink print fabric

1 fat quarter (18" × 22" [45.5 × 56 cm]) light green print fabric

1 fat eighth (9" × 22" [23 × 56 cm]) dark gray text fabric

¾ yd (68.5 cm) red print fabric

1¼ yd (1.1 m) dark green fabric

⅞ yd (80 cm) striped fabric

3¼ yd (3 m) backing fabric

57" × 58" (145 × 147.5 cm) batting

tools

Essential tool kit (page 13)

The striped fabric used in this design
helps define the central block and
provides a graphic punch for the binding.

cut the fabric

WOF = width of fabric

From light green print fabric:

○ cut 1 strip 4½" × 22"
(11.5 × 56 cm); crosscut into 4
squares 4½" × 4½" (11.5 × 11.5 cm)

○ cut 2 strips 2½" × 13½"
(6.5 × 34.5 cm)

○ cut 2 strips 2½" × 12½"
(6.5 × 31.5 cm)

From dark gray text fabric:

○ cut 2 squares 4½" × 4½"
(11.5 × 11.5 cm)

○ cut 2 rectangles 4½" × 5½"
(11.5 × 14 cm)

From red print fabric:

○ cut 1 strip 17" (43 cm) × WOF;
crosscut into 2 squares 17" × 17"
(43 × 43 cm)

○ cut 2 strips 3½" (9 cm) × WOF;
crosscut into 2 rectangles 3½" ×
13½" (9 × 34.5 cm) and 2 rectangles 3½" × 12½" (9 × 31.5 cm)

From dark green fabric:

○ cut 1 strip 17" (43 cm) × WOF;
crosscut into 2 squares 17"
× 17"
(43 × 43 cm)

○ cut 2 strips 6" (15 cm) × WOF;
crosscut into 2 rectangles 6"
× 13½"
(15 × 34.5 cm) and 2
rectangles 6" × 12½"
(15 × 31.5 cm)

○ cut 5 strips 2½" (6.5 cm)
× WOF

From striped fabric:

○ cut 2 strips 6" (15 cm) × WOF;
crosscut into 2 rectangles 6"
× 13½"
(15 × 34.5 cm) and 2
rectangles 6" × 12½"
(15 × 31.5 cm)

○ cut 6 strips 2½" (6.5 cm)
× WOF

From backing fabric, cut 2
rectangles 57" (145 cm) × WOF

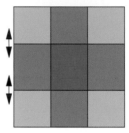

figure 1 (make 1)

figure 2 (make 2)

Make the Quilt Top

This quilt is created from one large-
scale churn dash block, composed
of units arranged in three rows of
three. For additional interest, the
central block is slightly rectangular
rather than square.

1 Sew a gray text rectangle to
each long edge of the pink print
rectangle to make the middle row of
the central nine-patch block. Press
each seam open. Sew light green
squares to opposite sides of a gray
text square; make two. Press the
seams open. Stitch a unit made from
squares to each long edge of the
unit made from rectangles to complete the nine-patch unit. Press the
seam allowances open **(FIGURE 1)**.

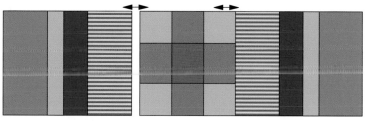

figure 3 (make 1)

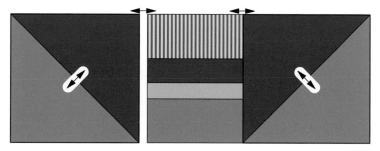

figure 4 (make 2)

2 Stitch the 13½" (34.5 cm) rectangles of striped, red, light green, and dark green fabrics together to make two striped units as shown (**FIGURE 2**). Press the seam allowances open. Each unit should measure 13½" × 16½" (34.5 × 42 cm). Sew the units to the long edges of the nine-patch unit as shown (**FIGURE 3**) and press all seams open.

3 Make four half-square triangle units (HSTs) from the 17" (43 cm) red and green squares (page 14). Press the seam allowances open and trim, if necessary, to measure 16½" × 16½" (42 × 42 cm). Stitch the 12½" (31.5 cm) rectangles of striped, red, light green, and dark green fabrics together to make two striped units as in step 2; these units will measure 12½" × 16½" (31.5 × 42 cm). Sew a HST unit to each side of a striped unit; make two (**FIGURE 4**). Press the seams open.

Half-Square Triangles ◤ Churn Dash! **53**

4 Referring to the **CONSTRUCTION DIAGRAM** (see right), sew the three pieced rows together. Add the 2½" (6.5 cm) dark green borders, following my method for measuring and assembling borders (page 17). Attach the top and bottom borders first, then the side borders. Press all seams open.

Finish the Quilt Top

5 Make a backing as desired, referring to Finishing Your Quilt (page 18) as needed. If you prefer, use your own techniques for the finishing steps; construct a pieced backing if you'd like.

6 Make a quilt sandwich from the backing, batting, and quilt top. Baste all layers together.

7 Quilt as desired, then trim the backing and batting to match the quilt top.

8 Stitch the 2½" (6.5 cm) striped binding strips together to form a continuous length. Bind the raw edges to finish the quilt.

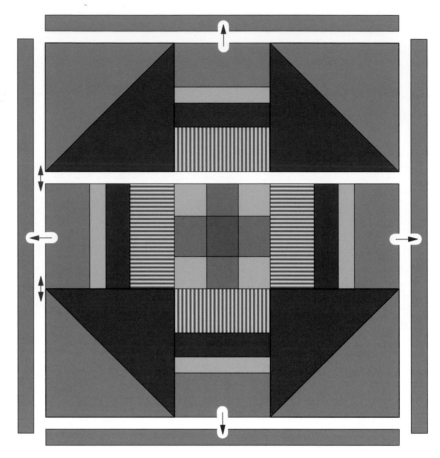

Construction Diagram

If you choose your fabrics carefully, you can also use prints for the background of this design. In this variation, the vibrant orange floral provides the contrast needed to tone down the lively pink print.

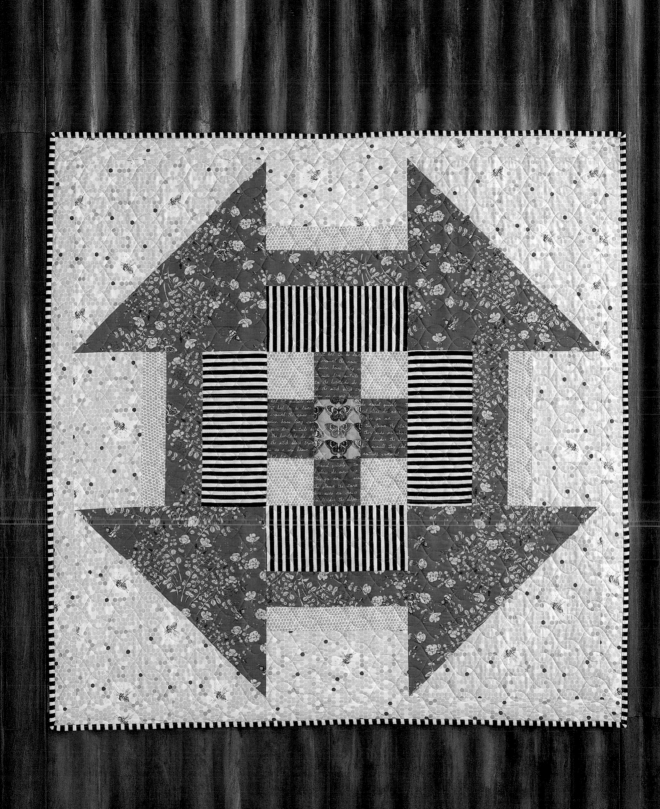

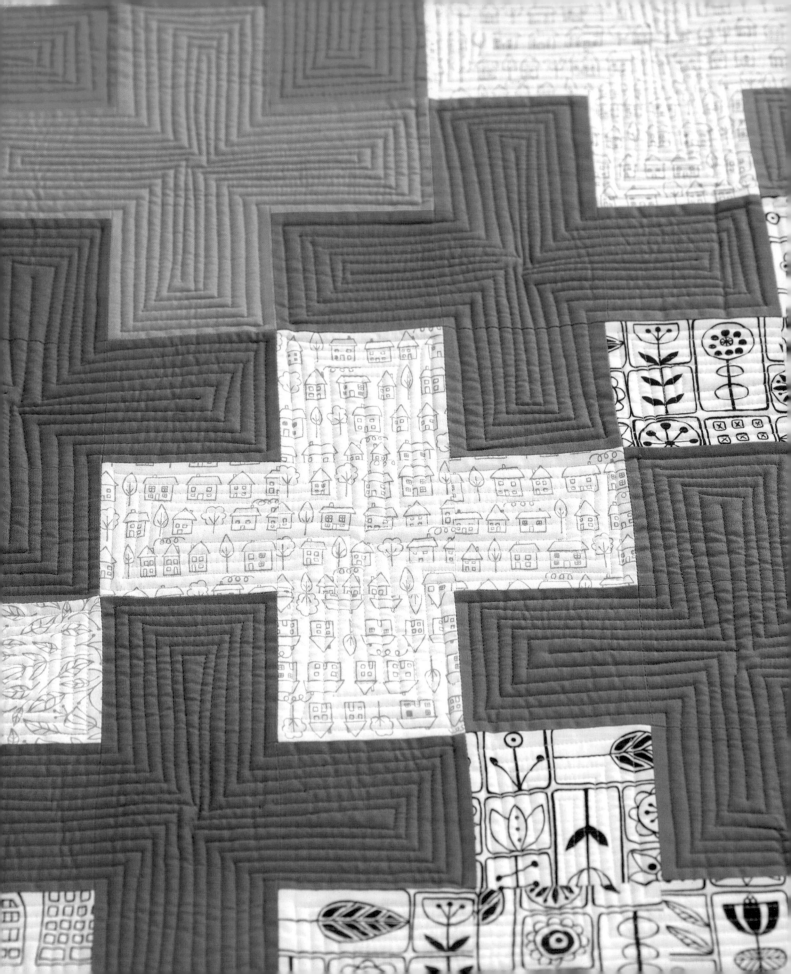

Crosses

4

Cross quilts are huge right now, popular with both modern and traditional quilters alike. And no wonder—the distinctive motifs seem to appear like magic during the construction of the quilt top. In addition to the projects, there are a couple of variations to show you how different color schemes and fabric choices can have a big impact on the final product.

◀ *Echo quilting from Lullaby, page 68*

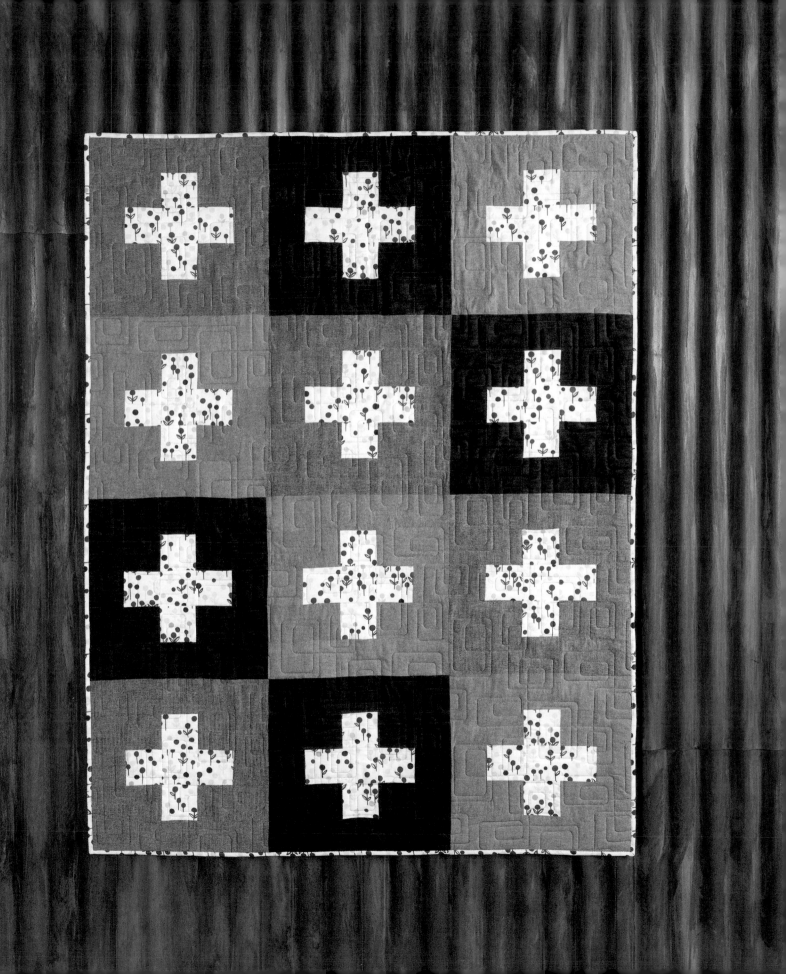

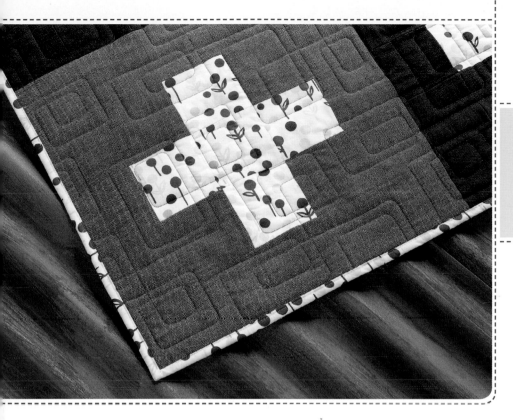

BLOCK SIZE: 17½" × 17½" (44.5 × 44.5 cm)

QUILT SIZE: 52½" × 70" (133.5 × 178 cm)

PIECED BY Siobhan Rogers

LONG-ARM QUILTED BY Kim Bradley

materials

All fabric amounts are for 45" (114.5 cm) wide fabric unless otherwise noted

1 yd (01.5 om) dark blue denim fabric

1⅞ yd (1.7 m) light blue denim fabric

1¼ yd (1.1 m) print fabric

3½ yd (3.2 m) backing fabric

61" × 78" (155 × 198 cm) batting

NOTES: *I've given fabric requirements for new denim yardage based on a useable width of 42" (106.5 cm), but denim is also sold in wider widths. Adjust the fabric requirements if you use wide denim. If your denim contains spandex, handle it with care so you don't stretch the blocks while you're cutting and sewing. Finally, you can achieve some slight variations in color by playing with the orientation of the denim's nap.*

tools

Essential tool kit (page 13)

Denim Crosses

Denim is one of those fabrics that can scare people, but with a little bit of preparation it can actually be wonderful to sew. It's nice and sturdy, rarely loses its shape, and looks great when quilted. Use a sharp jeans needle in your sewing machine and install a new blade on your rotary cutter for best results. Although this quilt was made with denim yardage, try using your old jeans—or thrift-shop jeans—for a great scrappy look.

cut the fabric

WOF = width of fabric

From dark blue denim fabric, cut 8 strips 4" (10 cm) × WOF; crosscut into 80 squares 4" × 4" (10 × 10 cm)

From light blue denim fabric, cut 16 strips 4" (10 cm) × WOF; crosscut into 160 squares 4" × 4" (10 × 10 cm)

From print fabric:

- ○ cut 6 strips 4" (10 cm) × WOF; crosscut into 60 squares 4" × 4" (10 × 10 cm)

- ○ cut 7 strips 2½" (6.5 cm) × WOF

From backing fabric, cut 2 rectangles 61" (155 cm) × WOF

Make the Blocks

1 Referring to the **BLOCK DIAGRAM** (see page 61), arrange the squares in blocks containing five rows of five squares. Sew the squares together in rows, then join the rows to make a block, matching all seams. Make four blocks with dark blue denim fabric and eight blocks with light blue denim fabric. (Remember that you can reverse the nap direction for fun if you'd like.) Press all seams open, not to the side, as the denim fabric is bulky.

If you'd prefer a brighter color palette, add more prints to the mix as shown in this variation.

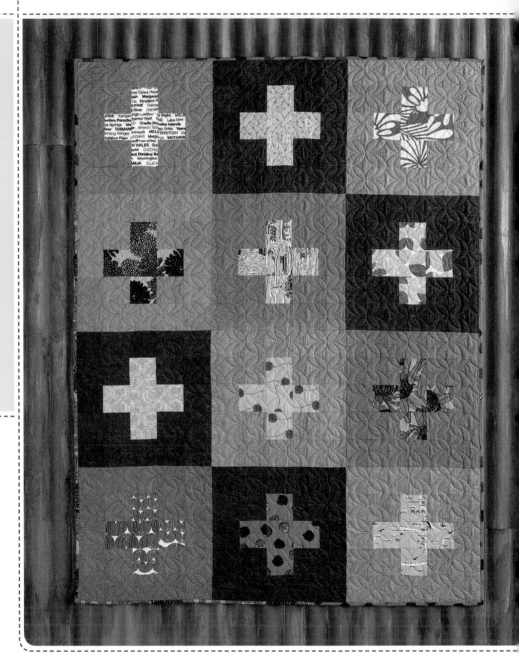

Make the Quilt Top

2 Following the **CONSTRUCTION DIAGRAM** (see page 61), arrange the blocks in four rows of three blocks each. Sew the blocks together in rows and press the seam allowances open. Stitch the rows together, matching the seams. Press all seams open.

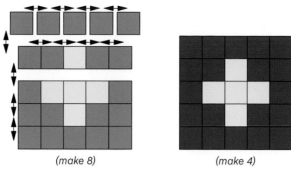

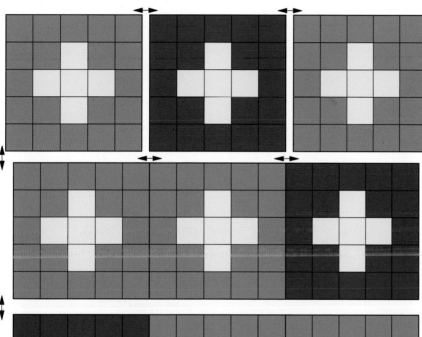

(make 8)   (make 4)

Block Diagram

Finish the Quilt

3 Make a backing as desired, referring to Finishing Your Quilt (page 18) as needed. Use your favorite methods for the finishing steps if you wish, including constructing a pieced backing.

4 Make a quilt sandwich from the backing, batting, and quilt top. Baste all layers together.

5 Quilt as desired, then trim the backing and batting to match the quilt top.

6 Join the 2½" (6.5 cm) print binding strips to form a continuous length. Bind the raw edges to finish the quilt.

 time-saver! With its big blocks, this pattern can be completed in a jiffy. But remember that jelly roll strips can be used for a super-quick binding, too, if you want to add more pop to the design by adding additional prints.

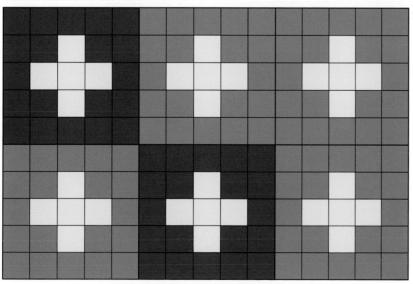

Construction Diagram

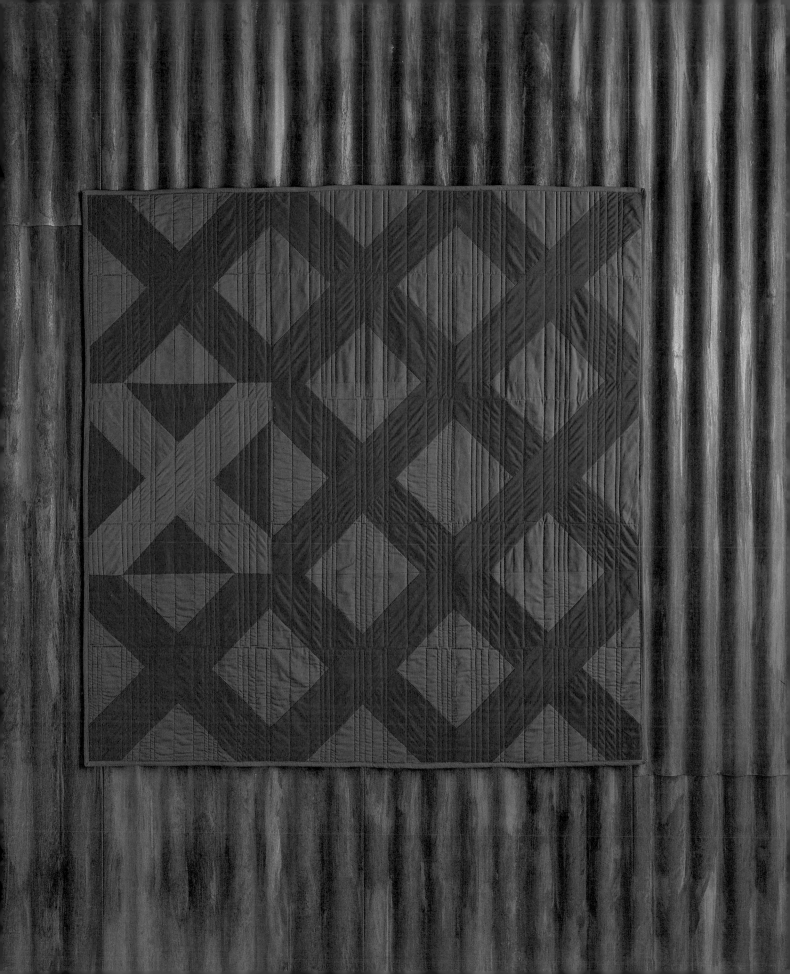

BLOCK SIZE: 17" × 17" (43 × 43 cm)

QUILT SIZE: 51" × 51" (129.5 × 129.5 cm)

PIECED BY Siobhan Rogers

LONG-ARM QUILTED BY Kim Bradley

Kisses and Hugs

materials

All fabric amounts are for 45" (114.5 cm) wide fabric unless otherwise noted

1¾ yd (1.6 m) purple fabric

2⅜ yd (2.2 m) red fabric

3⅜ yd (3.1 m) backing fabric

59" × 59" (150 × 150 cm) batting

tools

Essential tool kit (page 13)

I have signed my name with an "xx" at the end ever since I can remember, and I always loved finishing off all our Christmas cards with an "xoxo" as a kid. It was an introduction to abbreviations that stuck with me—how can something so small mean something so big? To me, presenting a quilt to someone means something big, too; it's like giving them a hug or a kiss—a small sign of affection with a higher purpose. If you need to show someone some love, a clever twist on half-square triangles helps this quilt come together quickly.

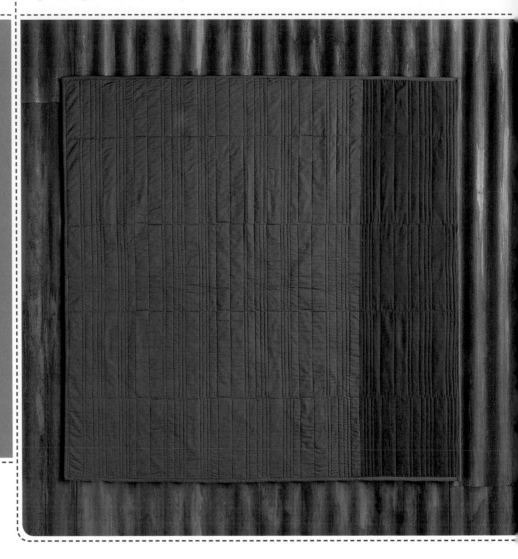

Combine the two fabrics used in the quilt design for a bold backing.

cut the fabric

WOF = width of fabric

From purple fabric:

- ○ cut 8 squares 12" × 12" (30.5 × 30.5 cm)

- ○ cut 1 rectangle 5" × 22" (12.5 × 56 cm)

- ○ cut 1 rectangle 5" × 26" (12.5 × 66 cm)

- ○ cut 6 strips 2½" (6.5 cm) × WOF

From red fabric:

- ○ cut 8 rectangles 5" × 22" (12.5 × 56 cm)

- ○ cut 8 rectangles 5" × 26" (12.5 × 66 cm)

- ○ cut 1 square 12" × 12" (30.5 × 30.5 cm)

From backing fabric, cut 2 rectangles 59" (150 cm) × WOF

Make the Block

1 Cut the 12" (30.5 cm) purple squares on the diagonal to form sixteen half-square triangles (HSTs). Fold the red 5" × 22" (12.5 × 56 cm) rectangles and purple HSTs in half to find the centers and press lightly. Align the centers of an HST and a rectangle, right sides together and raw edges matched **(FIGURE 1)**, and stitch. Press the seam open. Repeat to add a second HST to the opposite side of the rectangle **(FIGURES 2 AND 3)**. Trim the block to measure 14¾" × 14¾" (37.5 × 37.5 cm), using the pressed line as a guide for keeping the patchwork centered **(FIGURE 4)**.

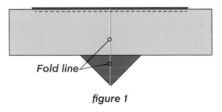

Fold line

figure 1

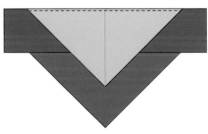

figure 2

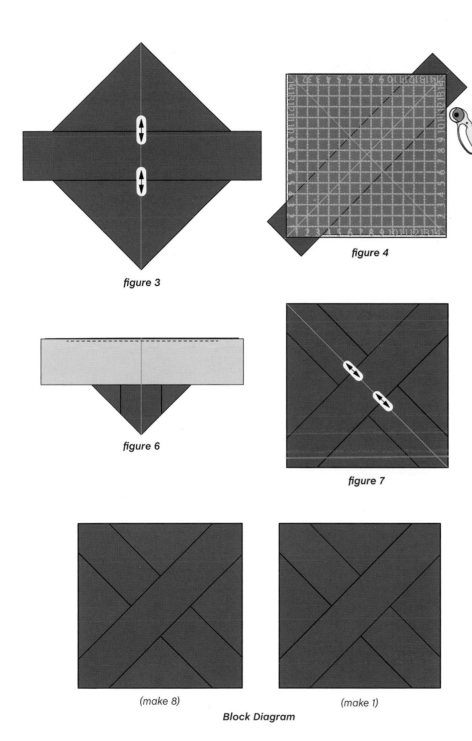

figure 3

figure 4

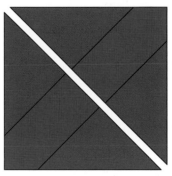

figure 5

figure 6

figure 7

(make 8)

(make 1)

Block Diagram

2 Cut the block on the diagonal along the centerline creases, perpendicular to the center rectangle, and piece a 5" × 26" (12.5 × 66 cm) rectangle into the center as in Step 1 (**FIGURES 5, 6, AND 7**). Be sure to keep the halves of the first red rectangle aligned. Trim the block to measure 17½" × 17½" (44.5 × 44.5 cm).

3 Repeat Steps 1 and 2 to make a total of eight blocks with red crosses.

4 Referring to the **BLOCK DIAGRAM** (see left), follow Steps 1–3 to make one block with the colors reversed, using the red square and the purple rectangles.

Make the Quilt Top

5 Referring to the **CONSTRUCTION DIAGRAM** (see page 66), arrange the squares in three rows of three blocks each, noting the position of the color-reversed block. Sew the

blocks together in rows, matching the seams where they meet. Press the seams open. Join the rows, aligning the seams, and stitch. Press the seam allowances open.

Finish the Quilt

6 Make a backing as desired, referring to Finishing Your Quilt (page 18) as needed. Feel free to use your favorite methods for the finishing steps, including constructing a pieced backing if you would like.

7 Make a quilt sandwich from the backing, batting, and quilt top. Baste all layers together.

8 Quilt as desired, then trim the backing and batting to match the quilt top.

9 Join the 2½" (6.5 cm) strips to form a continuous length of binding. Bind the raw edges to finish the quilt.

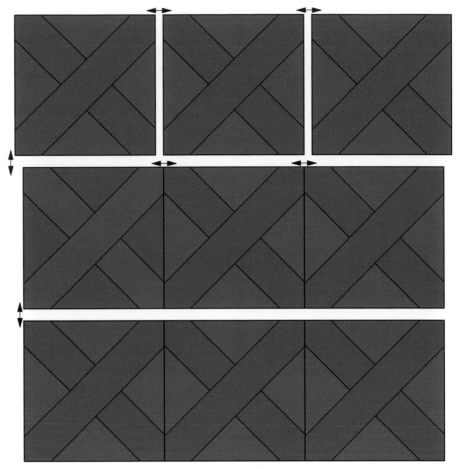

Construction Diagram

Sometimes variations can make a completely different statement; compare these versions of Kisses and Hugs to see how the prints in the variation capture the eye, while the red crosses in the featured version are dominant. Intriguing, isn't it?

BLOCK SIZE: 3½" × 3½" (9 × 9 cm)

QUILT SIZE: 35" × 42" (89 × 106.5 cm)

PIECED AND QUILTED BY Siobhan Rogers

materials

All fabric amounts are for 45" (114.5 cm) wide fabric unless otherwise noted

8 fat quarters (18" × 22" [45.5 × 56 cm]): 1 blue, 1 green, 2 pink, 1 red print, 1 blue print, 1 green print, 1 black print

1½ yd (1.4 m) backing fabric (see Note)

⅜ yd (34.5 cm) binding fabric

43" × 50" (109 × 127 cm) batting

NOTE: *If your fabric has less than 43" (109 cm) of useable width, you can make a pieced backing to provide additional width, or purchase 2⅞ yd (2.7 m) of fabric and cut two backing rectangles.*

tools

Essential tool kit (page 13)

Spray adhesive (optional)

Lullaby

The cross quilt is having a moment now, enjoying a resurgence in popularity. It's a great pattern for using up remnants, and the graphic design works for any age or gender. When I was planning this baby-sized project, I had a nice variety of prints in my stash but not enough of each to do a whole lot, so I added some complementary solids to the mix of fabrics. The large block size—and small quilt size—make this a good design for a gift that comes together quickly.

cut the fabric

WOF = width of fabric

From the blue fat quarter, cut
20 squares 4" × 4" (10 × 10 cm)

From the green fat quarter, cut
10 squares 4" × 4" (10 × 10 cm)

From the pink fat quarters, cut
40 squares 4" × 4" (10 × 10 cm)

From the red print fat quarter,
cut 11 squares 4" × 4" (10 × 10 cm)

From the blue print fat quarter,
cut 15 squares 4" × 4" (10 × 10 cm)

From the green print fat quarter,
cut 14 squares 4" × 4" (10 × 10 cm)

From the black print fat quarter,
cut 10 squares 4" × 4" (10 × 10 cm)

From the backing fabric, cut 1
rectangle 50" (127 cm) × WOF

From the binding fabric, cut
5 strips 2½" (6.5 cm) x WOF

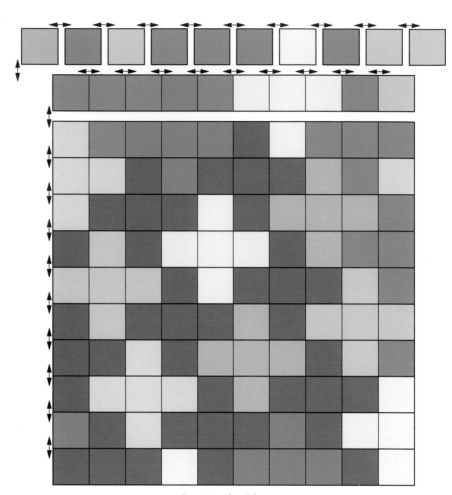

Construction Diagram

Make the Quilt Top

1 Each full cross is created by the arrangement of squares on the quilt top, but the quilt is built row by row. There are twelve rows of ten squares. See the Construction Diagram to arrange the squares in rows; organize each row for sewing by stacking the squares (page 13) and piece the rows together, pressing all seams open.

2 Sew the rows together in pairs, matching all seams. Press the seams open and then join the pairs to complete the quilt top. Press all seams open.

Finish the Quilt

3 Make a backing as desired, referring to Finishing Your Quilt (page 18) as needed. Unless your fabric is narrow, you'll need only one length of fabric for the backing of this quilt. Use your favorite methods for the finishing steps if you prefer, including constructing a pieced backing.

Echo quilting adds depth to the design and accentuates the cross motifs.

time-saver! Unlike most of the other quilts in *By the Block*, this quilt is built by clever arrangement of simple squares rather than assembling a number of blocks. It is an excellent example of how a basic piecing technique can result in a sophisticated design.

4 Make a quilt sandwich from the backing, batting, and quilt top. Baste all layers together. You may find that spray adhesive works well to quickly baste the layers of this small quilt.

5 Quilt as desired, then trim the backing and batting to match the quilt top. I chose to use matching thread and echo quilt each full cross as well as each partial cross. I began with the middle cross, working from the cross's outer edge to the center.

6 Join the binding strips to form a continuous length. Bind the raw edges to finish the quilt.

Triangles

5

Experiment with triangles and see just how easy it is to use this iconic shape in new and innovative ways. Each of these quilts is so different, you might be surprised they're all based on the same motif! Learn to cut triangles quickly and efficiently, add a fun border using offcuts, and create hexagons in a surprisingly simple way.

◄ *Detail of the quilting from Camouflage, page 86*

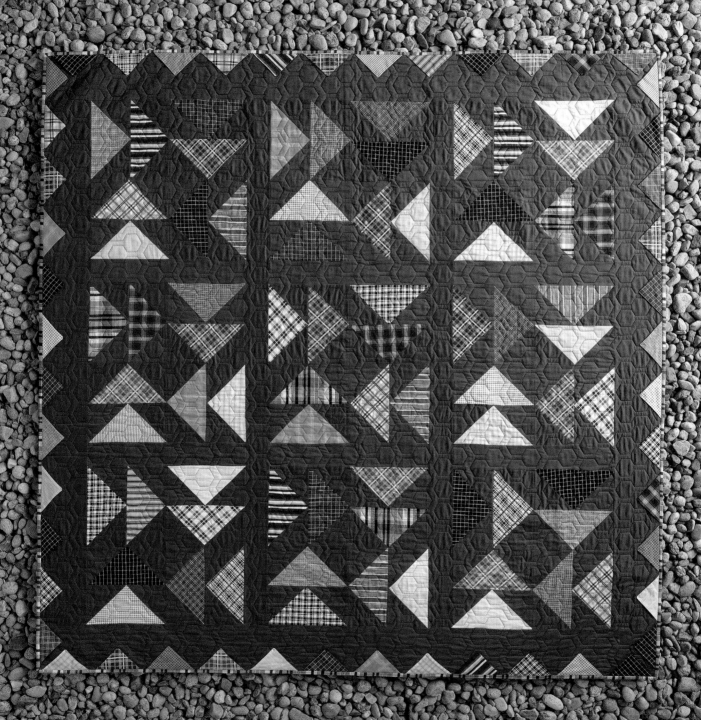

BLOCK SIZE: 20" × 20" (51 × 51 cm)

QUILT SIZE: 78" × 78" (198 × 198 cm)

PIECED BY Siobhan Rogers

LONG-ARM QUILTED BY Kim Bradley

Come Flying

I'd been saving up all my checks and plaids for a quilt. I drew up a few sketches, but nothing grabbed me—I was struggling with how to use a variety of busy checks and plaids without creating a mess that makes you go cross-eyed! Then I came across the traditional Flying Dutchman block, and it was the perfect solution. The triangles on the border are made from the Flying Geese offcuts, so very little fabric goes to waste.

materials

All fabric amounts are for 45" (114.5 cm) wide fabric unless otherwise noted

¼ yd (23 cm) each of 27 different checked, plaid, and striped fabrics

5½ yd (5 m) dark gray fabric

4⅞ yd (4.5 m) backing fabric

¾ yd (68.5 cm) checked binding fabric

86" × 86" (218 × 218 cm) batting

tools

Essential tool kit (page 13)

cut the fabric

WOF = width of fabric

From each checked, plaid, and striped fabric, cut 1 strip 5½" (14 cm) × WOF; crosscut into 3 rectangles 10½" × 5½" (26.5 × 14 cm)

From dark gray fabric:

○ cut 21 strips 5½" (14 cm) × WOF; crosscut into 144 squares 5½" × 5½" (14 × 14 cm)

○ cut 6 strips 3½" (9 cm) × WOF; crosscut into 6 strips 20½"

(52 cm) long. Join the offcuts and crosscut into 2 strips, 66½" (169 cm) long, from the assembled fabric. (If your fabric is narrow, you may need to cut an additional strip.)

○ cut 8 strips 6½" (16.5 cm) × WOF

From checked binding fabric, cut 9 strips 2½" (6.5 cm) × WOF

From backing fabric, cut 2 rectangles 86" (218 cm) × WOF

fyi

You'll cut eighty-one rectangles but only use seventy-two in the quilt; I used the nine extra rectangles in the pieced backing. Keep forty-eight of the triangle offcuts you trim away when you make the Flying Geese units—these will be used along the border of the quilt.

Make the Block

1 Make Flying Geese units for the large Flying Dutchman blocks. Begin by drawing a diagonal line from corner to corner on the wrong side of each gray 5½" (14 cm) square. Place a marked square on one end of a checked, plaid, or striped rectangle with right sides together, matching the raw edges. Sew along the marked diagonal line (**FIGURE 1**).

2 Trim the excess fabric ¼" (6 mm) outside the stitching line; remember to keep the two triangle offcuts to use later (**FIGURE 2**).

3 Press the seam open and press the gray triangle outward. Add another gray square to the opposite edge of the patterned fabric and stitch, trim, and press as in Steps 1–3 (**FIGURE 3**).

4 Repeat Steps 1–3 to make seventy-two Flying Geese units.

5 Referring to the **BLOCK DIAGRAM** (see page 77), stitch eight Flying Geese units together to form one block. Make nine blocks.

Make the Quilt Top

6 Arrange the blocks in three rows of three blocks as shown in the **CONSTRUCTION DIAGRAM** (see page 78). Position a 3½" × 20½" (9 × 52 cm) gray sashing strip between each pair of blocks in each row. Sew the blocks and sashing strips together in rows. Press the seams open.

7 Join the three rows together with the 3½" × 66½" (9 × 169 cm) gray sashing strips. Press the seams open.

8 Use the 6½" (16.5 cm) gray strips to measure and attach a border, using my method (page 17). Press the seams open.

figure 1

figure 2

figure 3

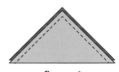

figure 4

figure 5

tips

Plaids and checks are often off-grain. If you want your fabric pattern to appear straight and aligned to the grain, you'll need to buy extra fabric for a bit of fussy cutting. I must confess that it doesn't bother me—I like the imperfection that may result. As far as solids go, make sure to consistently use the same side of the fabric as the right side, or you may see differences in shade.

Finish the Quilt

9 Make a backing as desired, referring to Finishing Your Quilt (page 18) as needed. Feel free to use your favorite methods for the finishing steps, including constructing a pieced backing if you'd like.

10 Make a quilt sandwich from the backing, batting, and quilt top. Baste all layers together.

11 Quilt as desired, then trim the backing and batting to match the quilt top.

12 Use the offcuts from the Flying Geese units to add the decorative triangles to the borders. Place a gray triangle and a patterned triangle right sides together. Sew around two sides of the triangle, leaving the long edge open **(FIGURE 4)**.

13 To reduce bulk, trim away the little tip of the triangle above the seams, leaving about ⅛" (3 mm) **(FIGURE 5)**. Turn the triangle right side

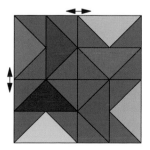

Block Diagram

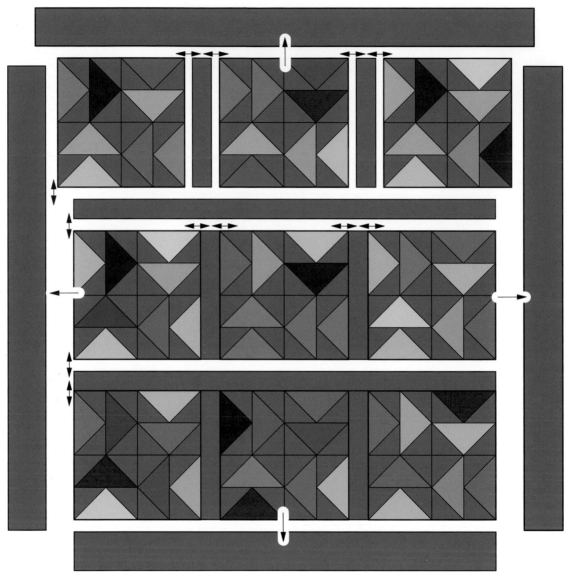

Construction Diagram

out and press flat. Pin the triangles around the outside of the quilt, aligning the unfinished edges with the edge of the quilt top and positioning twelve triangles per side. Play around with the spacing until you're happy, then baste using a scant ¼" (6 mm) seam.

14 Join the binding strips to form a continuous length. Bind the raw edges to finish the quilt and attach the decorative triangles. Take a few stitches by hand or machine through the tip of each triangle to secure it to the quilt and prevent floppiness.

This scrappy backing is reminiscent of work from the Gee's Bend quilters. Work as they did and use the materials you have on hand to finish the quilt.

BLOCK SIZE: 17⅛" × 14⅞" (43.5 × 38 cm)

QUILT SIZE: 89½" × 102" (227.3 × 259 cm)

PIECED BY Siobhan Rogers

LONG-ARM QUILTED BY Kim Bradley

materials

*All fabric amounts are for 45"
(114.5 cm) wide fabric unless
otherwise noted*

6¼ yd (5.7 m) white fabric

1 yd (91.5 cm) each of 2 different navy
print fabrics

⅜ yd (34.5 cm) each of 2 different
aqua print fabrics

¼ yd (23 cm) yellow print fabric

¼ yd (23 cm) lavender print fabric

⅜ yd (34.5 cm) white print fabric

8¼ yd (7.6 m) backing fabric

98" × 110" (249 × 279 cm) batting

NOTE: *This quilt is especially suited for
a pieced backing, because it's just a
little too wide to make from two fabric
lengths. If you piece a strip from
leftovers to add to the backing, you'll
need only two 98" (249 cm) lengths,
or 5½ yd (5 m), instead of 8¼ yd
(7.6 cm)—a considerable savings
in fabric.*

tools

Essential tool kit (page 13)

Template A (see insert)
(or 60° triangle ruler-optional)

Template plastic or paper for cutting
Template A

Paper for trapezoid pattern

Prism

Lots of my ideas come from art and surface design.
One of my favorite designers released a great
wrapping paper featuring roughly drawn triangles;
I promptly bought it and taped a sheet to my
studio wall. I studied it for a while to decide how
to translate that lively design into the quilt pattern
you see here.

Notice how the large pieced
triangles are simply inverted
to create the overall design.

cut the fabric

WOF = width of fabric

CUTTING NOTES: Use Template A to cut triangles from the 3¾" (9.5 cm) strips, alternating point-up and point-down placement to use the fabric efficiently **(FIGURE 1)**. If you use a 60º triangle ruler instead, follow the manufacturer's instructions to cut triangles with a finished height of 3" (7.5 cm). Cut extra triangles, if desired, for flexibility in arranging the colors. On paper, draw a trapezoid shape using the dimensions in **FIGURE 2**. Add ¼" (6mm) seam allowance to each edge of the shape. Cut out the pattern and use it for cutting the trapezoids as directed below.

From each navy print fabric, cut 9 strips 3¾" (9.5 cm) × WOF; from these strips cut 143 triangles from each fabric

From each aqua print fabric, cut 3 strips 3¾" (9.5 cm) × WOF; from these strips cut 37 triangles from each fabric

From yellow print fabric, cut 2 strips 3¾" (9.5 cm) × WOF; from these strips cut 30 triangles

From purple print fabric, cut 2 strips 3¾" (9.5 cm) × WOF; from these strips cut 30 triangles

From white print fabric, cut 3 strips 3¾" (9.5 cm) × WOF; from these strips cut 45 triangles

From white fabric:

○ cut 17 strips 3¾" (9.5 cm) × WOF; from these strips cut 285 triangles

○ cut 10 strips 2½" (6.5 cm) × WOF

○ cut 11 strips 1½" (3.8 cm) × WOF

○ cut 2 strips 16" (40.5 cm) × WOF; use the pattern created from Figure 2 to cut 6 trapezoids and 6 reversed trapezoids from the strips

○ cut 3 strips 2½" (6.5 cm) × WOF

○ cut 5 strips 15" (38 cm) × WOF

From backing fabric, cut 3 rectangles 98" (249 cm) × WOF

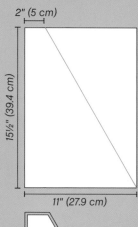

figure 1

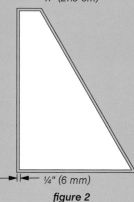

2" (5 cm)

15½" (39.4 cm)

11" (27.9 cm)

¼" (6 mm)

figure 2

Make the Triangles

1 I prefer to assemble one large triangle at a time so that I can design the units individually, but you can speed up the process by assembling strips ahead of time, then assembling the strips into pleasing blocks. To prepare strips, make the following:

○ 30 strips of 9 triangles (5 print and 4 white)

○ 30 strips of 7 triangles (4 print and 3 white)

○ 30 strips of 5 triangles (3 print and 2 white)

○ 15 strips of 3 triangles (3 navy print)

○ 15 strips of 3 triangles (2 print and 1 white)

time-saver! Remember that you can stack strips to cut multiple triangles at once. It will save you lots of time on this project.

2 To assemble the blocks, refer to the **BLOCK DIAGRAMS**; place a navy print triangle at the top of each Block A and place a single navy print triangle and a row of three navy print triangles at the top of each Block B.

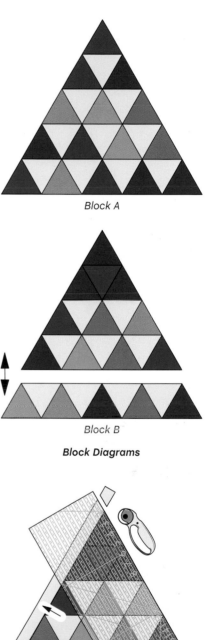

Block A

Block B

Block Diagrams

figure 3

Make the Quilt Top

Refer to the **CONSTRUCTION DIAGRAM (PAGE 85)** as reference for Steps 3–8.

③ Use the white 1½" (3.8 cm) strips to join the pieced triangles into rows. To begin, sew a length of sashing strip to the left side of a triangle, press the seams toward the sashing strip, and trim the top of the strip as shown **(FIGURE 3)**.

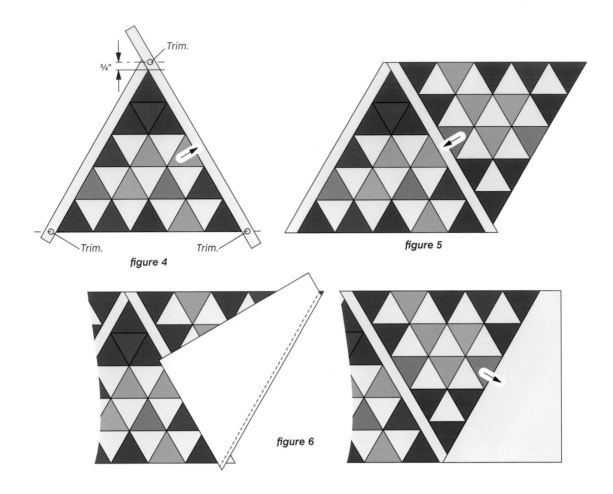

figure 4

figure 5

figure 6

4 Sew a length of sashing strip to the opposite side of the triangle and press the seams toward the sashing strip. Trim the sashing strips ¾" (2 cm) above the point of the triangle, parallel to the triangle's base **(FIGURE 4)**. Trim both sashing strips even with the base of the pieced triangle.

5 Sew a second pieced triangle in the reverse orientation to the opposite side of the sashing strip as shown, matching the base of the new triangle to the trimmed edge of the sashing. Press the seams toward the sashing strip **(FIGURE 5)**. Continue the process in Steps 3 to 5 to complete a row of five triangle blocks, alternating Blocks A and B. Make six rows, three containing three A blocks and three containing three B blocks.

Arrange the rows as shown in the **CONSTRUCTION DIAGRAM**.

6 Stitch a trapezoid or reversed trapezoid to each end of every row. Press the seam allowances toward the trapezoids **(FIGURE 6)**.

7 Measure the width of the triangle rows and make sashing strips from the 1½" (3.8 cm) white strips to fit, using my method for measuring and constructing borders (page 17).

8 Measure and construct narrow borders from the 2½" (6.5 cm) white strips. Sew them to the top and bottom of the quilt. Measure and assemble the side borders from the 15" (38 cm) white strips and add them to the quilt top.

Finish the Quilt

9 Make a backing as desired, referring to Finishing Your Quilt (page 18) as needed; see the Note on page 81 if you prefer to make a pieced backing. Use your favorite methods for the finishing steps if you wish.

10 Make a quilt sandwich from the backing, batting, and quilt top. Baste all layers together.

11 Quilt as desired, then trim the backing and batting to match the quilt top.

12 Join the remaining 2½" (6.5 cm) white strips to form a continuous length. Use it to bind the raw edges and finish the quilt.

Construction Diagram

HEXAGON SIZE: 17¼" × 20¼" (44 × 51.5 cm)

QUILT SIZE: 60¾" × 70" (154.5 × 178 cm)

PIECED BY Siobhan Rogers

LONG-ARM QUILTED BY Angela Walters

Camouflage

Inspiration comes from the oddest places! The idea for this quilt came from a graphic icon in a magazine ad. This particular design reminded me of camouflage, as I purposely made the hexagons tricky to see by dividing them into triangles and using alternating colors to hint at the hexagonal shapes. Custom quilting within the hexagons helps differentiate the units, but you could make the hexagons more obvious by changing the color palette.

materials

All fabric amounts are for 45" (114.5 cm) wide fabric unless otherwise noted

24 fat quarters (18" × 22" [45.5 × 56 cm]): 12 in different pink prints and 12 in different blue prints

3⅞ yd (3.6 m) backing fabric

⅝ yd (57 cm) binding fabric

69" × 78" (175 × 198 cm) batting

tools

Essential tool kit (page 13)

cut the fabric

WOF = width of fabric

From each pink fat quarter, cut 2 strips, 10" × 18" (25.5 × 45.5 cm); crosscut into 6 rectangles, 10" × 5⅞" (25.5 × 15 cm). Cut the rectangles in half from corner to corner to form triangles **(FIGURE 1)**, cutting three rectangles of each fabric in each direction as shown.

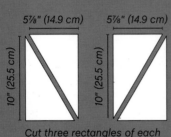

5⅞" (14.9 cm)   5⅞" (14.9 cm)

10" (25.5 cm)   10" (25.5 cm)

Cut three rectangles of each pink print in each direction.

Cut two rectangles of each blue print in each direction.

figure 1

From each blue fat quarter, cut 2 strips, 10" × 18" (25.5 × 45.5 cm); crosscut into 4 rectangles, 10" × 5⅞" (25.5 × 15 cm). Cut the rectangles in half from corner to corner to form triangles **(FIGURE 1)**, cutting two rectangles of each fabric in each direction as shown.

From backing fabric, cut 2 rectangles 69" (175 cm) × WOF

From binding fabric, cut 7 strips 2½" (6.5 cm) × WOF

fyi

This pattern isn't difficult, but if you're new to sewing triangles, be aware that they can stretch or lose shape because one side is cut on the bias. I suggest choosing a sturdy, stable fabric for this quilt. You'll have extra half-rectangle triangles (HRTs) to use for piecing the back or another project.

* **tip**

If you've wanted to make a hexagon quilt but are intimidated by Y-seams, this is the project for you. Assembling the pieced hexagons requires only straight seams!

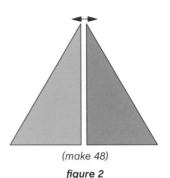

(make 48)

figure 2

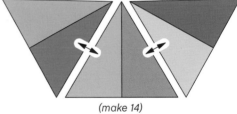

(make 14)

figure 3

Make the Hexagon

1 Beginning with the pink fabrics, sew pairs of HRTs—one cut in each direction—together **(FIGURE 2)**. Press the seam allowances open. Make forty-eight triangular units. Join three triangular units to make a half-hexagon unit **(FIGURE 3)**. Press the seams open and trim the dog-ears. Make two half-hexagons at a time, using each of the twelve fabrics only once as shown **(FIGURE 4)**. Make fourteen half-hexagon units. Sew a single HRT to one side of a remaining triangular unit to make a quarter hexagon; make six, three with the single HRT on the right and three with the single HRT on the left **(FIGURE 5)**.

2 Repeat Step 1 with the blue fabrics, beginning with forty triangular units. Sew ten blue half-hexagon units. Make ten blue quarter-hexagon units, five with the single HRT on the right and five with the single HRT on the left.

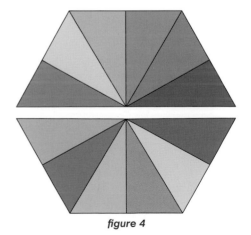

figure 4

Notice the many different quilting patterns used within the hexagons; they add more energy to the design.

Make the Quilt Top

3 Referring to the **CONSTRUCTION DIAGRAM** (see page 90), arrange the units into eight horizontal rows on your design wall. You'll see the full hexagonal shapes form when the rows are adjacent to one another; play with the arrangement of the half-hexagon units so each fabric appears no more than once in each full hexagon, as much as possible. When you're satisfied with the arrangement, sew the units into eight rows. Press each seam open.

4 Sew the rows together, working carefully so the center points of the hexagons join precisely. Press the seams open.

Finish the Quilt

5 Make a backing as desired, referring to Finishing Your Quilt (page 18) as needed. Feel free to use your favorite methods for the finishing steps; remember that you'll have extra HRTs if you'd like to make a pieced backing.

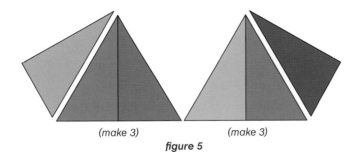

(make 3)   (make 3)

figure 5

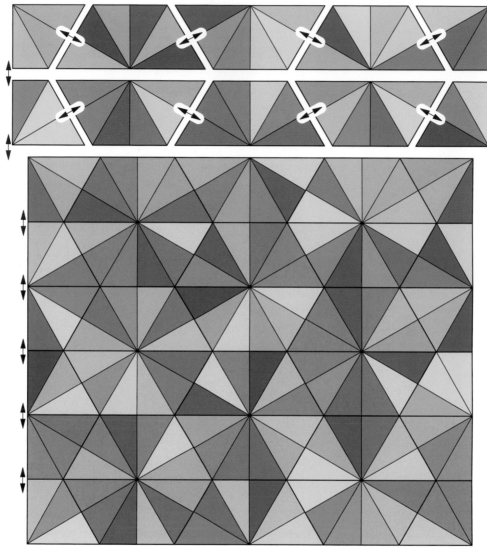

Construction Diagram

6 Make a quilt sandwich from the backing, batting, and quilt top. Baste all layers together.

7 Quilt as desired, then trim the backing and batting to match the quilt top.

8 Join the 2½" (6.5 cm) binding strips to form a continuous length. Bind the raw edges to finish the quilt.

If you prefer to purchase some yardage instead of using only fat quarters for this design, you can use the leftovers to piece a simple backing.

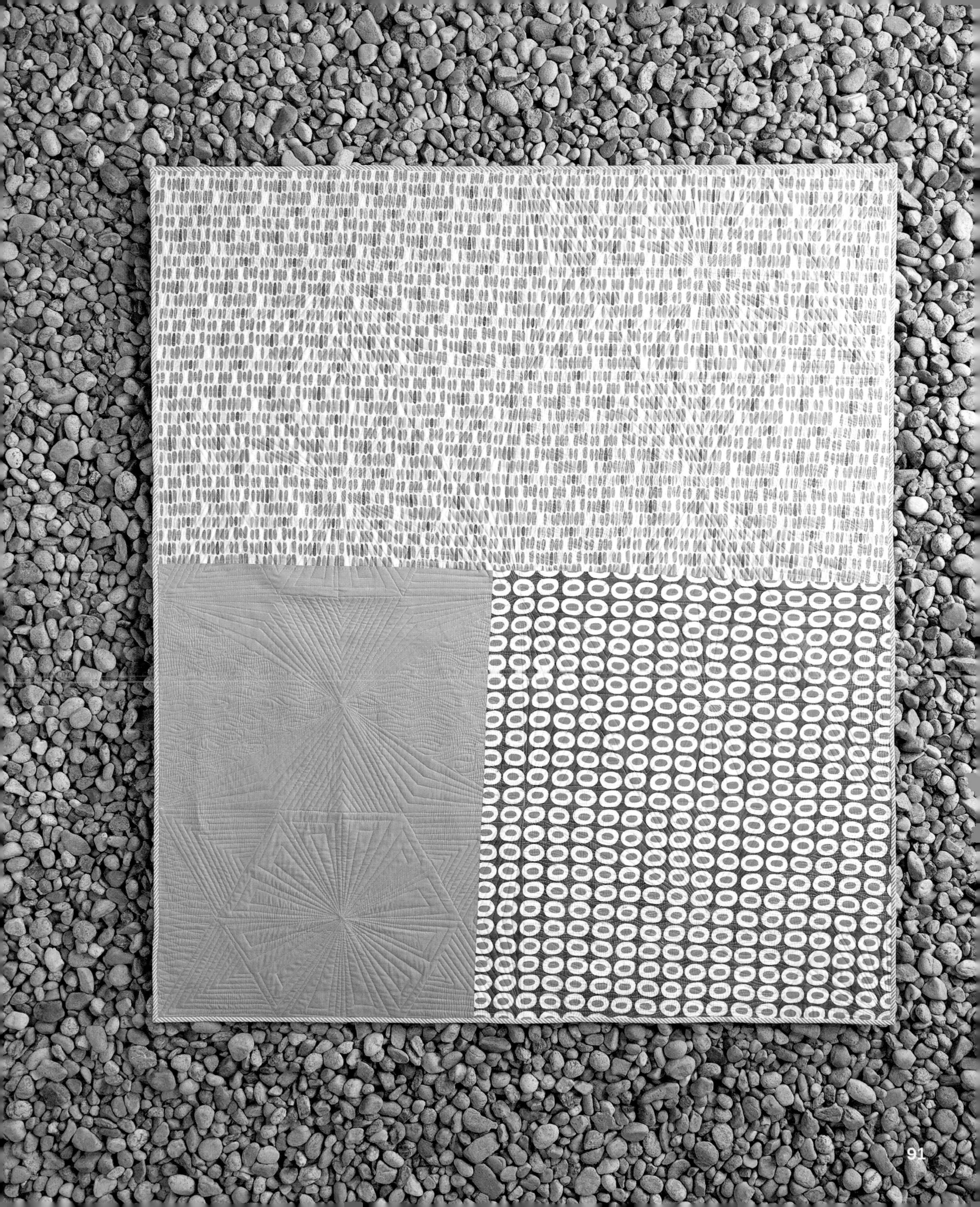

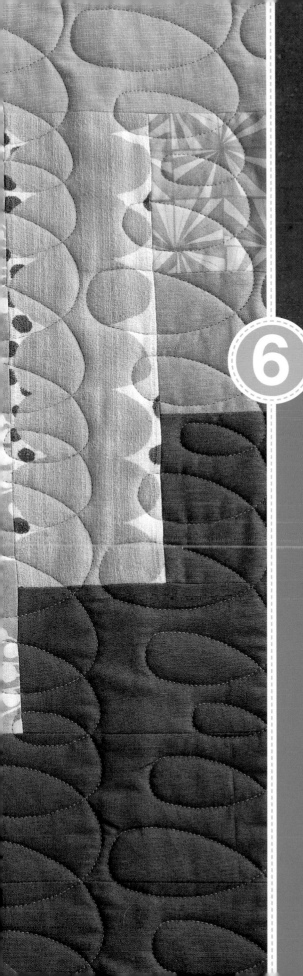

Log Cabin

6

Is there a more recognizable quilt pattern than the Log Cabin? This arrangement of simple shapes still offers so many possibilities for design that it's a joy to revisit again and again. In this collection of quilts, the pattern is turned upside down, sideways . . . and worked up in linen for a sophisticated take on this classic motif.

◄ *Fabrics used in Color Burst,*
page 98

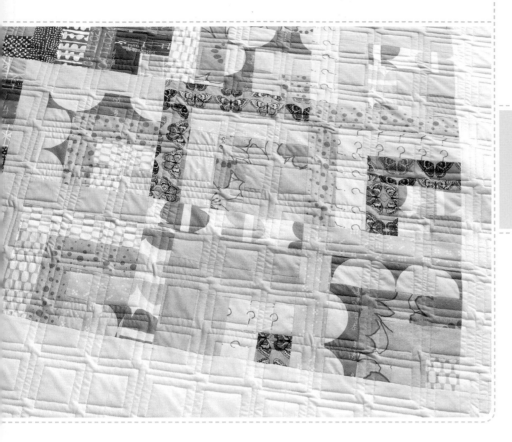

BLOCK SIZE: 10" × 10" (25.5 × 25.5 cm)

QUILT SIZE: 56½" × 63¾" (143.5 × 162 cm)

PIECED BY Siobhan Rogers

LONG-ARM QUILTED BY Kim Bradley

Deco

This quilt was inspired by a trip to Los Angeles, when I looked at all the wonderful old Art Deco buildings with their graphic shapes and opulent colorways of golds, blacks, and grays. I wanted to create a quilt that looked like a stained-glass window, and this half-square variation of the traditional Log Cabin pattern fit perfectly with my theme. The long-arm quilting reflects the diagonal squares and adds to the architectural nature of the quilt.

materials

All fabric amounts are for 45" (114.5 cm) wide fabric unless otherwise noted

3 yd (2.7 m) white fabric

One 2½" (6.4 cm) × WOF strip from each of 14 different yellow fabrics

One 2½" (6.4 cm) × WOF strip from each of 12 different gray fabrics

3⅝ yd (3.4 m) backing fabric

65" × 72" (165 × 183) batting

tools

Essential tool kit (page 13)

cut the fabric

WOF = width of fabric

From white fabric:

○ cut 8 strips 10½" (26.5 cm) × WOF; crosscut into 32 squares, 10½" × 10½" (26.5 × 26.5 cm)

○ cut 7 strips 2½" (6.5 cm) × WOF

From the yellow strips, cut a total of 8 squares, 2½" × 2½" (6.5 × 6.5 cm) (see fyi)

From the gray strips, cut a total of 5 squares, 2½" × 2½" (6.5 × 6.5 cm) (see fyi)

From backing fabric, cut 2 rectangles 65" (165 cm) × WOF

fyi

Reserve the remainder of the yellow and gray strips for Log Cabin piecing.

 time-saver! Are you a jelly roll fan? Although you wouldn't need an entire roll of either the gray or the yellow fabrics to make this quilt, you might look for one roll of precut strips that features both colors; it would not only speed up the construction of this quilt but also make it economical.

Make the Blocks

1 Make half-square Log Cabin blocks (page 15) for this quilt, beginning with a 2½" (6.5 cm) square in one corner. Follow the **BLOCK DIAGRAM** (see page 97) to create a total of eight yellow and five gray blocks, varying the fabrics in each individual block. Press all seams open.

Make the Quilt Top

2 Referring to the **CONSTRUCTION DIAGRAM**, arrange the Log Cabin and white blocks in diagonal rows. Join the blocks in rows, pressing the seam allowances open. Stitch the rows together, matching the seam intersections and pressing each seam open.

3 Trim the quilt top into a rectangle **(FIGURE 1)**. The trim line falls ¼" (6 mm) from the outer seam intersections to provide a seam allowance for the binding **(FIGURE 2)**.

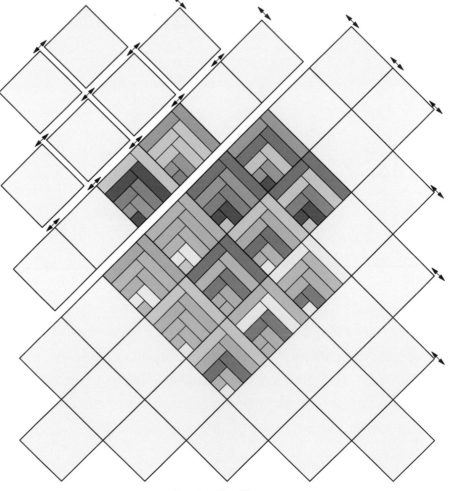

Construction Diagram

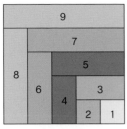

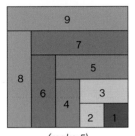

(make 8)

(make 5)

Block Diagram

figure 1

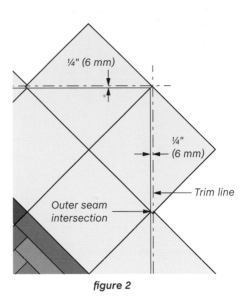

¼" (6 mm)

¼"
(6 mm)

Outer seam
intersection

Trim line

figure 2

Finish the Quilt

4 Make a backing as desired, referring to Finishing Your Quilt (page 18) as needed. Feel free to use your favorite methods for the finishing steps, including constructing a pieced backing if you would like.

5 Make a quilt sandwich from the backing, batting, and quilt top. Baste all layers together.

6 Quilt as desired, then trim the backing and batting to match the quilt top.

7 Join the 2½" (6.5 cm) white binding strips to form a continuous length. Bind the raw edges to finish the quilt.

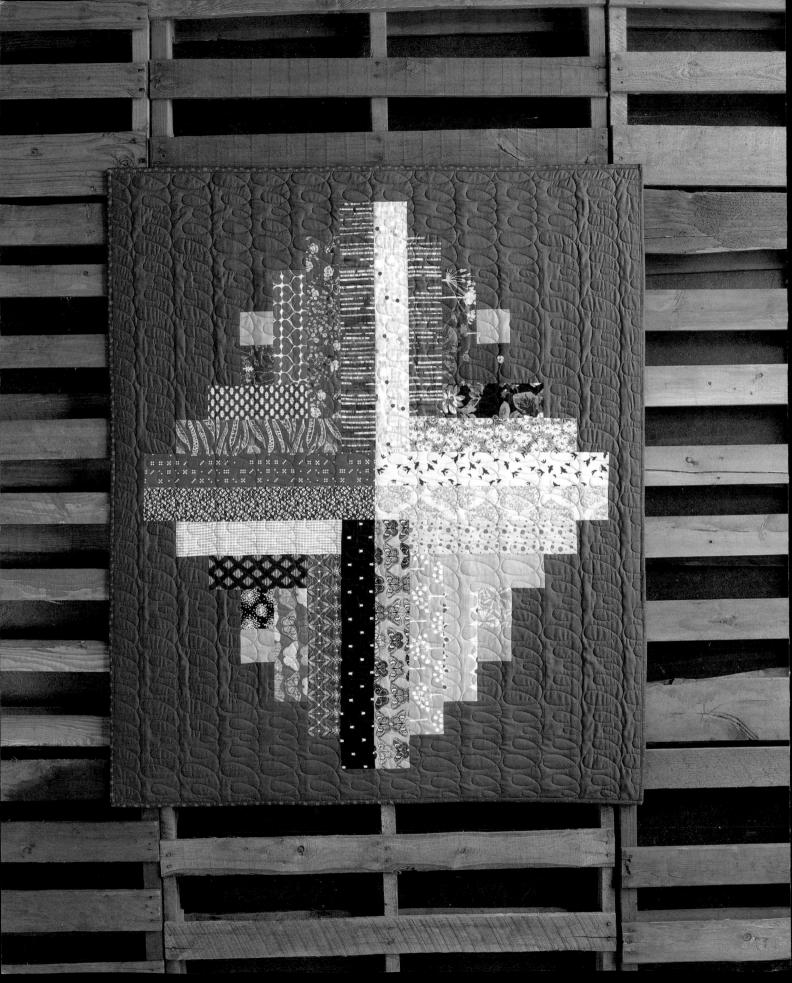

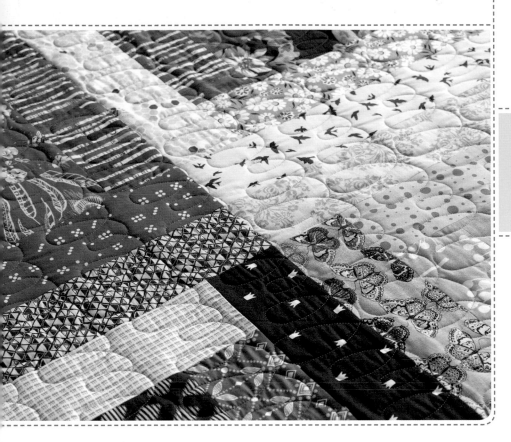

BLOCK SIZE: 24" × 28" (61 × 71 cm)

QUILT SIZE: 48" × 56" (122 × 142 cm)

PIECED BY Siobhan Rogers

LONG-ARM QUILTED BY Kim Bradley

materials

All fabric amounts are for 45" (114.5 cm) wide fabric unless otherwise noted

1¾ yd (1.6 m) medium gray fabric

⅛ yd (11.5 cm) light gray fabric

⅛ yd (11.5 cm) each of 7 different blue fabrics

⅛ yd (11.5 cm) each of 7 different yellow fabrics

⅛ yd (11.5 cm) each of 7 different red fabrics

⅛ yd (11.5 cm) each of 7 different purple fabrics

3⅛ yd (2.9 m) backing fabric

½ yd (45.5 cm) binding fabric

56" × 64" (142 × 162.5 cm) batting

tools

Essential tool kit (page 13)

Color Burst

I've admired old, complex Log Cabin quilts for a long time, and I wanted to design a simple quilt that looked as complicated as some of the old quilts yet would come together quickly. I also wanted to play with color—this design reminds me of an artist's palette covered with splats of paint! Choose a variety of cheerful prints to play against the neutral gray fabric.

cut the fabric

WOF = width of fabric

From medium gray fabric, cut 16 strips 3½" (9 cm) × WOF; from these strips, crosscut a total of:

○ 4 rectangles 3½" × 4"
  (9 × 10 cm)

○ 4 rectangles 3½" × 9½"
  (9 × 24 cm)

○ 4 rectangles 3½" × 10½"
  (9 × 26.5 cm)

○ 4 rectangles 3½" × 15½"
  (9 × 39.5 cm)

○ 4 rectangles 3½" × 16½"
  (9 × 42 cm)

○ 4 rectangles 3½" × 21½"
  (9 × 54.5 cm)

○ 4 rectangles 3½" × 22½"
  (9 × 57 cm)

○ 4 rectangles 3½" × 28½"
  (9 × 72.5 cm)

From light gray fabric, cut 1 strip 3½" (9 cm) × WOF; crosscut into 4 squares 3½" × 3½" (9 × 9 cm)

From each blue, yellow, red, and purple fabric, cut 1 strip 3½" (9 cm) × WOF; from these strips, cut the following for each colorway, using each print only once:

○ 1 rectangle 3½" × 4" (9 × 10 cm)

○ 1 rectangle 3½" × 9½"
  (9 × 24 cm)

○ 1 rectangle 3½" × 10½"
  (9 × 26.5 cm)

○ 1 rectangle 3½" × 15½"
  (9 × 39.5 cm)

○ 1 rectangle 3½" × 16½"
  (9 × 42 cm)

○ 1 rectangle 3½" × 21½"
  (9 × 54.5 cm)

○ 1 rectangle 3½" × 22½"
  (9 × 57 cm)

From backing fabric, cut 2 rectangles 56" (142 cm) × WOF

From binding fabric, cut 6 strips 2½" (6.5 cm) × WOF

fyi

You'll have some excess fabric from the strips; use it in a pieced backing if you'd like.

Make the Block

1 Refer to the **BLOCK DIAGRAMS** for the basic assembly of each block; construct each block as shown. When you sew pieces 2 and 3 to the central square, be sure to align and sew along the 3½" (9 cm) edges. This is what gives the blocks their rectangular shape, rather than a traditional square. Pieces 4 and 5 are 10½" (26.5 cm) long, while pieces 6 and 7 are just 9½" (24 cm) long. You'll follow this pattern of longer strips before shorter strips throughout the block assembly. There should be no need to trim any of the rectangular pieces during the assembly process. Press the seams open.

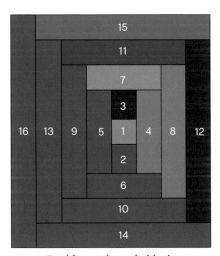

For blue and purple blocks

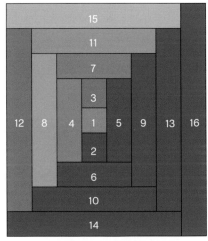

For yellow and red blocks

Block Diagrams

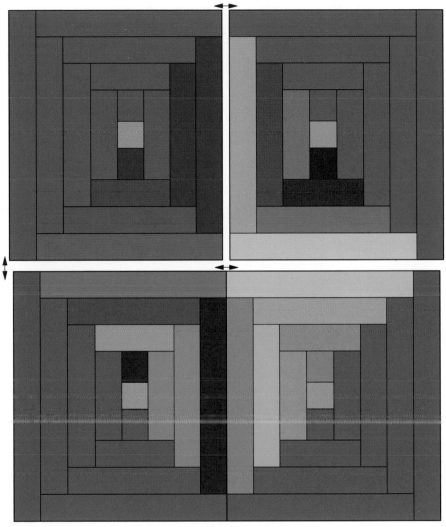

Construction Diagram

Make the Quilt Top

2 Arrange the four blocks as shown in the **CONSTRUCTION DIAGRAM**. Sew two blocks together to make each row, matching intersecting seams. Press the seams open. Join the rows to make the quilt; press the seam allowances open.

Finish the Quilt

3 Make a backing as desired, referring to Finishing Your Quilt (page 18) as needed. Feel free to use your favorite methods for the finishing steps, including constructing a pieced backing if you would like—you'll have some remnants to work with.

4 Make a quilt sandwich from the backing, batting, and quilt top. Baste all layers together.

5 Quilt as desired, then trim the backing and batting to match the quilt top.

6 Sew the binding strips together to form a continuous length. Bind the raw edges to finish the quilt.

The leftover strips from the quilt top can be combined to make a vibrant backing. It's hard to say which side is more engaging!

time-saver! Set the iron up nearby—with so many short seams to sew (and press), it makes the blocks come together much more quickly.

This is a fun, versatile pattern. See how the same prints used in the featured quilt play out against a background of neutral print fabrics in this variation.

BLOCK SIZE: 27½" × 27½" (70 × 70 cm)

QUILT SIZE: 55" × 55" (139.5 × 139.5 cm)

PIECED BY Siobhan Rogers

LONG-ARM QUILTED BY Krista Withers

materials

All fabric amounts are for 45" (114.5 cm) wide fabric unless otherwise noted

2⅜ yd (2.2 m) salmon linen fabric

⅜ yd (34.5 cm) natural linen fabric

1" (2.5 cm) × WOF strips from at least 15 different print fabrics (35 strips total)

4" × 6" (10 × 15 cm) rectangles of several different print fabrics (10 rectangles total)

3½ yd (3.2 m) backing fabric

½ yd (45.5 cm) binding fabric

63" × 63" (160 × 160 cm) batting

tools

Essential tool kit (page 13)

1¼ yd (1.1 m) paper-backed fusible web

Liberty & Linen

This combination of fabrics reminds me of the quilts from the 1930s. I'm not sure whether it's the combination of the salmon solid with floral prints or the appliqué. Do you have a stash of fabric scraps? Use them in this quilt. Because the material I used (Liberty of London Tana Lawn) is a lovely but expensive fabric, I keep every little bit to use in quilts such as this one. If you don't have fabric scraps that you can use, how about buying some fat eighths?

cut the fabric

WOF = width of fabric

LOF = length of fabric

From salmon linen fabric:

○ cut 1 strip 28" (71 cm) × LOF; crosscut into 3 squares 28" × 28" (71 × 71 cm)

○ cut 1 strip 14¼" (36 cm) by LOF; crosscut into 2 rectangles 14¼" × 28" (36 × 71 cm)

From natural linen fabric, cut 1 strip 11½" (29 cm) × WOF; crosscut into 5 rectangles 7½" × 11½" (19 × 29 cm)

From backing fabric, cut 2 rectangles 63" (160 cm) × WOF

From binding fabric, cut 6 strips 2½" (6.5 cm) × WOF

Make the Block

1 Trim each 4" × 6" (10 × 15 cm) rectangle into a diamond, connecting the midpoints of the sides to mark the cutting lines **(FIGURE 1)**.

2 Refer to the **DIAMOND DIAGRAM** (see page 107) to construct ten print diamonds in log-cabin style, using the 1" (2.5 cm) strips to surround the central diamond. Use the same print on two adjacent sides of the diamond, trimming each strip even with the diamond edge as it is added; switch to a new print for the next two sides. Continue until the central diamond is surrounded by three rounds of strips. Press all seams away from the central diamond as you work.

2" (5 cm)

3" (7.5 cm)

figure 1

3¾" (9.5 cm)

5¾" (14.5 cm)

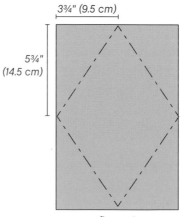

figure 2

time-savers! If you use Liberty of London Tana Lawn fabrics, I recommend using spray starch to iron the narrow strips so they are more stable to work with. Also, be sure to install a new, sharp needle and use a straight stitch plate to keep the corners from being drawn into the feed dogs. If you don't have a straight stitch plate, use a piece of scrap fabric as a leader when chain piecing.

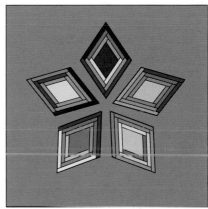

(make 2)

3 Cut the five natural linen rect-angles into diamonds, using the same method as in Step 1 **(FIGURE 2)**.

4 Using one of the linen diamonds as a pattern, cut fifteen pieces of the fusible web. Apply fusible web to the backs of all fifteen diamonds (ten log-cabin pieced diamonds and five natural linen diamonds). Trim the outer edges of each pieced diamond so the outer logs measure ½" (1.3 cm) wide, matching the other logs in the block. Trim ¼" (6 mm) from the outer edges of the linen diamonds to match the size of the pieced diamonds.

5 Referring to the **BLOCK DIAGRAMS**, arrange five dia-monds into a flower composition on each 28" (71 cm) square of linen

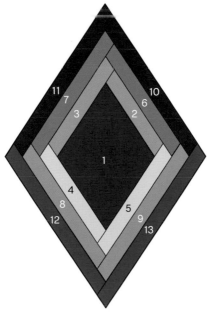

Diamond Diagram

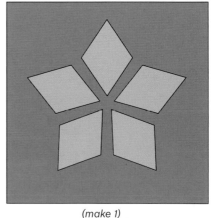

(make 1)
Block Diagrams

and fuse in place. The diamonds' points should be about 1" (2.5 cm) from the center of the linen square and spaced about 1¼" (3.2 cm) apart. After fusing, machine-stitch around each appliqué to secure the edges. This quilt is straight-stitched 1/16" (2 mm) from the raw edges; switch to a zigzag, blanket, or other stitch if you prefer. Make two blocks with the log-cabin diamonds and one block with the linen diamonds.

Make the Quilt Top

6 Referring to the **CONSTRUCTION DIAGRAM**, stitch the rectangular salmon blocks to the top and bottom edges of one log-cabin block, pressing the seams open. Stitch the remaining two blocks together, pressing the seam allowances open. Join the two units and press the seam open.

Finish the Quilt

7 Make a backing as desired, referring to Finishing Your Quilt (page 18) as needed. Use your favorite methods for the finishing steps if you prefer, including constructing a pieced backing.

8 Make a quilt sandwich from the backing, batting, and quilt top. Baste all layers together.

9 Quilt as desired, then trim the backing and batting to match the quilt top.

10 Join the 2½" (6.5 cm) binding strips to form a continuous length. Bind the raw edges to finish the quilt.

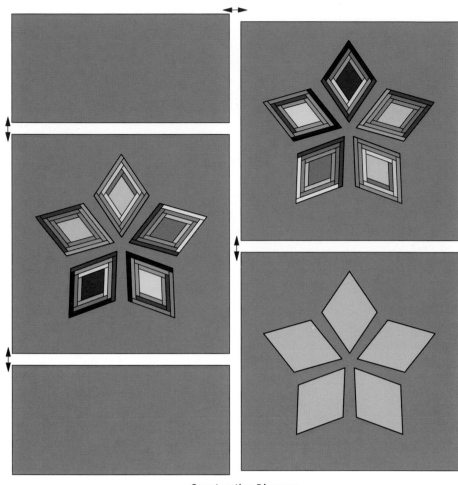

Construction Diagram

While I added some prints to piece a backing, this quilting would be beautiful on a solid-colored expanse of fabric.

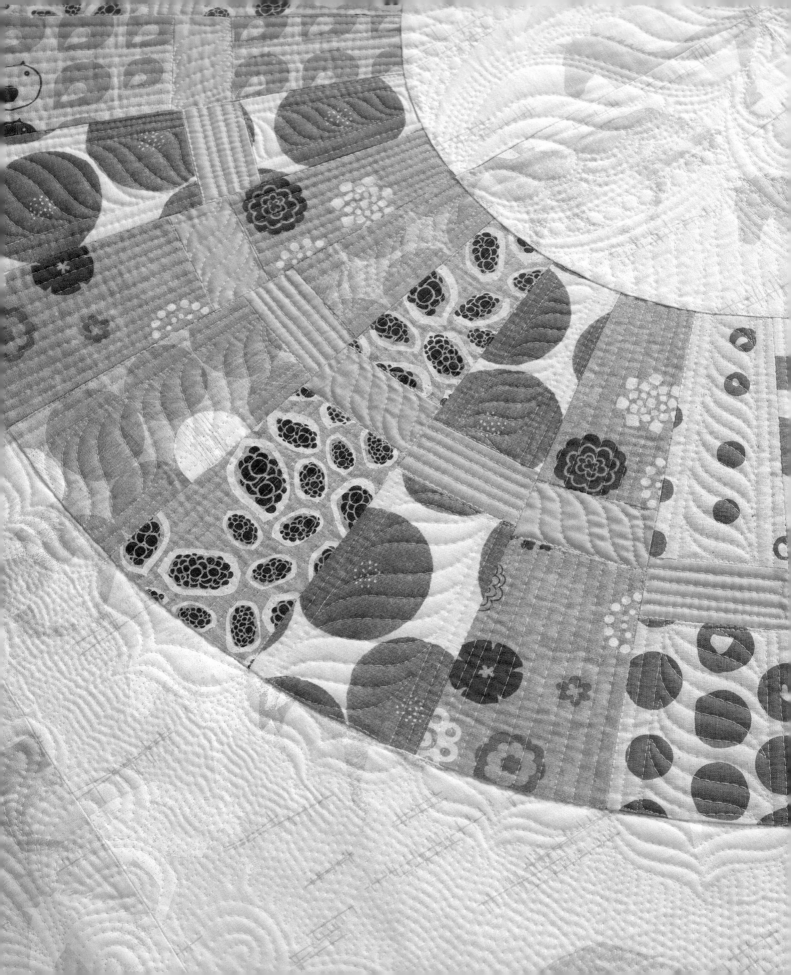

Curved Piecing

7

Have no fear—these patterns take a minimalist approach to curved piecing that yields maximum results. Each quilt offers the opportunity to add skills to your repertoire, because all offer a little something extra in addition to piecing curves. Learn to work with directional prints, for example, or use a smart technique that insures crisp curves when adding sashing.

◄ *Detail of wonky circle motif in Wild Horses, page 118*

Trinity

When I was a kid, my favorite number was three; it had a little to do with the fact that it was just my mum, dad, and me in our family. It also had a little to do with a childhood trip to Ireland when we explored Newgrange, the prehistoric monument just north of Dublin in the Boyne Valley. Since then I've always loved the Celtic triple spiral symbol. And I generally like the rule of odd numbers when arranging designs, so Trinity it is.

BLOCK SIZE: 12" × 12" (30.5 × 30.5 cm)

QUILT SIZE: 60" × 72" (152.4 × 182.9 cm)

PIECED BY Siobhan Rogers

LONG-ARM QUILTED BY Kim Bradley

materials

All fabric amounts are for 45" (114.5 cm) wide fabric unless otherwise noted

5 yd (4.6 m) natural linen fabric

12 jelly roll strips, each a different red fabric

3⅞ yd (3.6 cm) backing fabric

⅝ yd (57 cm) binding fabric

68" × 80" (173 × 203 cm) batting

NOTE: *Jelly rolls are packages of precut fabric strips, each 2½" × 44" (6.5 × 112 cm). They are usually sold as a collection of forty coordinating prints. Different fabric manufacturers and individual quilt shops may offer the same size strips under different names. You can also cut your own 2½" (6.5 cm) × WOF strips from fabrics of your choice.*

tools

Essential tool kit (page 13)

Templates A and B (see insert)

Template plastic or paper

cut the fabric

WOF = width of fabric

From natural linen, cut 10 strips 12½" (31.5 cm) × WOF; crosscut into 30 squares 12½" × 12½" (31.5 × 31.5 cm)

From binding fabric, cut 7 strips 2½" (6.5 cm) × WOF

From backing fabric, cut 2 rectangles 68" (173 cm) × WOF

Make the Block

1 Sew three red strips together to make a strip set; make four strip sets. Press the seams open. Crosscut each strip set into twelve segments, each 6½" × 3½" (16.5 × 9 cm), for a total of forty-eight segments (**FIGURE 1**).

2 Join four segments, one from each strip set, together along their long edges, matching the seams (**FIGURE 2**). Press the seams open. Make twelve units. Stitch two units together to form a square and press the seams open. Make six squares.

3 Arrange the squares as shown in **FIGURE 3**, alternating the orientation of the small rectangles. This will make for easier piecing later, as only the center seams will need to align when the squares are stitched together.

4 Use **TEMPLATE A** to cut two quarter circles from each red square, positioning the template on diagonally opposite corners of the square (**FIGURE 4**).

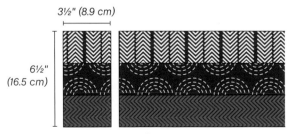

3½" (8.9 cm)

6½" (16.5 cm)

figure 1

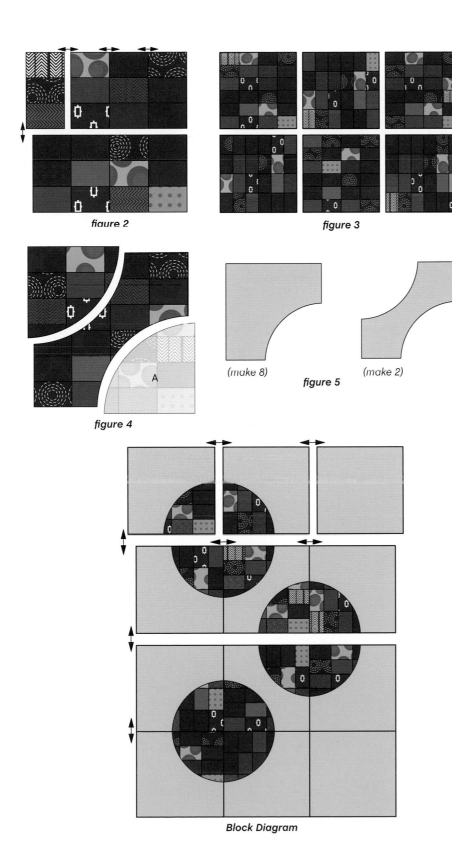

figure 2

figure 3

figure 4

(make 8)   (make 2)

figure 5

Block Diagram

tip

Because this quilt is based on a grid of large blocks, it's a versatile template for making variations. You could easily add more circles to this design or change the arrangement of the circles; it would be fun to play with the color of the circles, too.

5 Use **TEMPLATE B** to cut quarter circles from one corner of ten linen squares, as shown **(FIGURE 5)**. Set aside eight of the trimmed squares. Shift the template to cut another quarter circle from the diagonally opposite corner of each of the two remaining trimmed squares, again referring to **FIGURE 5**. Stabilize both the red quarter circles and the curved edges of the trimmed squares by staystitching a scant ¼" (6 mm) from the curved edges.

6 Be careful to arrange and assemble the blocks as shown in the **BLOCK DIAGRAM**, rotating quarter circles that will be sewn together as explained in Step 3. Stitch the red quarter circles to the trimmed linen squares, referring to curved piecing (page 16) as needed. Stitch each row together, then join the rows to complete the design. Press the seams open as you sew.

Make the Quilt Top

7 Referring to the **CONSTRUCTION DIAGRAM**, use the remaining linen squares to make border units for the quilt. Assemble two rows of three linen squares and two rows of six linen squares, pressing the seams open. Sew the short units to the top and bottom of the quilt center. Add the long units to the sides of the quilt.

Finish the Quilt

8 Make a backing as desired, referring to Finishing Your Quilt (page 18) as needed. Feel free to use your favorite methods for the finishing steps, including constructing a pieced backing if you'd like.

9 Make a quilt sandwich from the backing, batting, and quilt top. Baste all layers together.

10 Quilt as desired, then trim the backing and batting to match the quilt top.

11 Join the binding strips to form a continuous length. Bind the raw edges to finish the quilt.

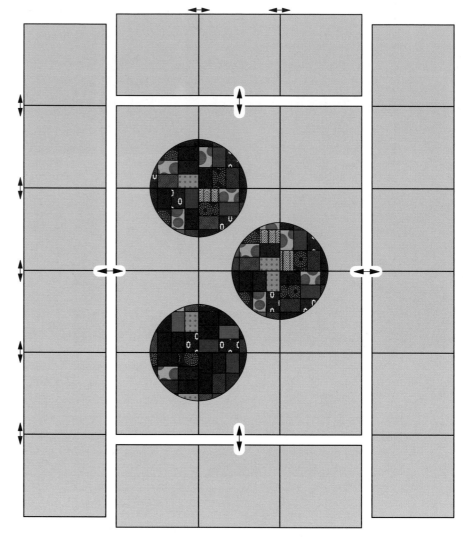

Construction Diagram

Use fabrics that are light in value for the quilt backing to maintain the quiet elegance of the quilt top.

BLOCK SIZE: 24½" × 24½" (62 × 62 cm)

QUILT SIZE: 69" × 69" (175 × 175 cm)

PIECED BY Siobhan Rogers

LONG-ARM QUILTED BY Angela Walters

Wild Horses

I had been eyeing this fabric for a while, though it can sometimes be difficult to use a medium- or large-scale print, especially when it's directional. I decided that I wanted all the horses to be upright, which means I couldn't always cut the fabric from selvedge to selvedge. I had to think about the best way to cut the fabric without too much waste. To tie the colors together, I used teal for the wonky circle and for the binding.

materials

All fabric amounts are for 45" (114.5 cm) wide fabric unless otherwise noted

9 fat quarters (18" × 22" [45.5 × 56 cm]): 2 different pink prints; 3 different gray prints; 1 white print; 2 different mustard prints, 1 teal solid

4 yd (3.6 m) medium-scale directional print fabric

4⅜ yd (4 m) backing fabric (see Notes on page 120)

⅝ yd (57 cm) binding fabric

77" × 77" (195.5 × 195.5 cm) batting

tools

Essential tool kit (page 13)

Templates A, B, and C (see insert)

Template plastic or paper.

cut the fabric

WOF = width of fabric

From each print fat quarter, cut 1 strip 6" to 7" (15 to 18 cm) × 22" (56 cm) and 1 strip 12" to 13" (30.5 to 33 cm) × 22" (56 cm). Vary the widths of the print strips to create the wonky teal circle in the finished quilt top.

From the teal fat quarter, cut 8 strips 2" × 22" (5 × 56 cm)

From directional print fabric (see Cutting Diagram):

○ cut 2 strips 10" × 60" (25.5 × 152.5 cm) on the lengthwise grain

○ cut 4 strips 10" (25.5 cm) × WOF

○ cut 2 of piece A and 2 of piece B

○ cut 2 of piece A reversed and 2 of piece B reversed

From backing fabric, cut 2 rectangles 77" (195.5 cm) × WOF

From binding fabric, cut 8 strips 2½" (6.5 cm) × WOF

fyi

This print is a linen-cotton blend; I love working with linen with its subtle color palette. Linen is sometimes a little wider than the usual bolts of quilter's cottons, so you may need less fabric than is suggested here if you use a wide linen. Also, I suggest adding 7" (18 cm) to each side when calculating backing for this project, which will require 4¾ yd (4.4 m) of backing fabric.

Make the Block

1 Sew a teal strip between two strips cut from the same print fat quarter **(FIGURE 1)**. Make eight strip sets; press the seams open.

2 Using template C, cut four wedges from each strip set. Divide the wedges into four groups, with one wedge of each print per group. Each group will form a quarter of the large circle.

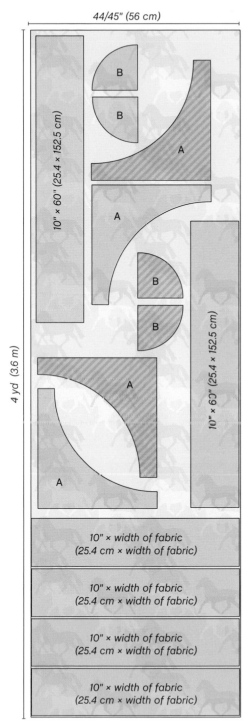

Cutting Diagram

44/45" (56 cm)

4 yd (3.6 m)

10" × 60" (25.4 × 152.5 cm)

10" × 60" (25.4 × 152.5 cm)

B
B
A
A
B
B
A
A

10" × width of fabric
(25.4 cm × width of fabric)

10" × width of fabric
(25.4 cm × width of fabric)

10" × width of fabric
(25.4 cm × width of fabric)

10" × width of fabric
(25.4 cm × width of fabric)

figure 1

figure 2

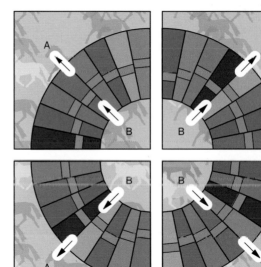

Block Diagram

3️⃣ Arrange the four groups on your design wall to make sure you like the arrangement of the wonky lines. When you're happy with the arrangement, stitch eight wedges together to make a quarter circle **(FIGURE 2)**. Make four quarter circles; press the seams open.

4️⃣ Stitch one A and one B to each quarter circle as in the **BLOCK DIAGRAM**, noting the direction of the background print as you stitch the pieces together. (See Curved Piecing on page 16.) Press the seams away from the center of the quilt. Make four blocks as shown; trim and square each block.

Piecing can be done on a large scale to make a backing, as seen on Wild Horses.

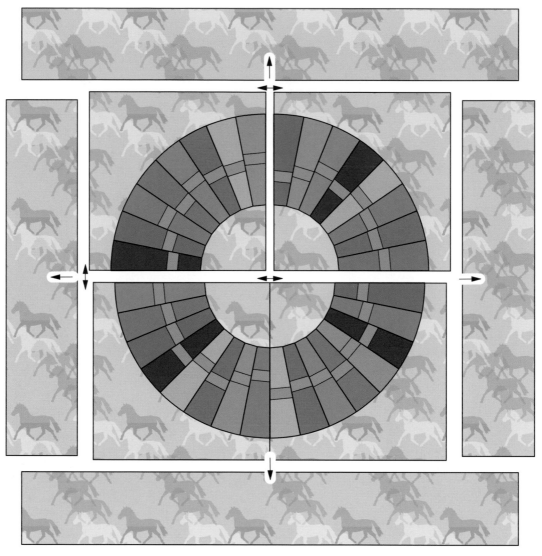

Construction Diagram

Make the Quilt Top

5 Refer to the **CONSTRUCTION DIAGRAM** and join the blocks together, matching the seams. Add the 10" (25.5 cm) borders, referring to my technique for measuring and constructing borders as needed (page 17). Sew the lengthwise-cut border strips to the side edges first, then add the assembled widthwise borders to the top and bottom.

Finish the Quilt

6 Make a backing as desired, referring to Finishing Your Quilt (page 18) as needed. Use your favorite methods for the finishing steps if you prefer, including constructing a pieced backing.

7 Make a quilt sandwich from the backing, batting, and quilt top. Baste all layers together.

8 Quilt as desired, then trim the backing and batting to match the quilt top.

9 Join the 2½" (6.5 cm) binding strips to form a continuous length. Bind the raw edges to finish the quilt.

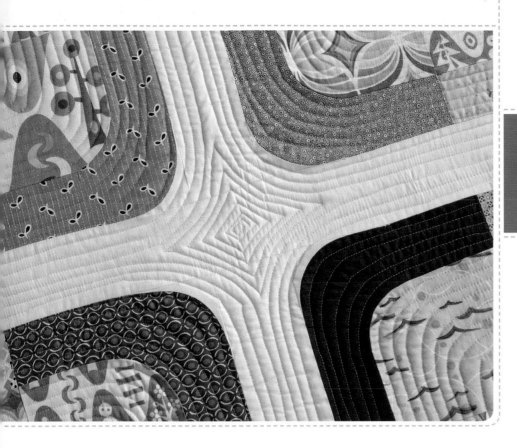

materials

All fabric amounts are for 45" (114.5 cm) wide fabric unless otherwise noted

12 fat eighths (9" × 22" [23 × 56 cm]): 4 large-scale prints, 4 different pink prints, and 4 different blue prints

1⅛ yd (1 m) white fabric

1½ yd (1.4 m) backing

⅜ yd (34.5 cm) binding fabric

40" × 51" (101.5 × 129.5 cm) batting

tools

Essential tool kit (page 13)

Templates A, B, and C (see insert)

Template plastic or paper

Polaroid

How great is a Polaroid photo? As a kid, I loved the excitement of waiting for the film to develop and remember the laughter as the image would start to appear. This quilt develops quickly too, with only four large blocks and easy curved piecing. The curved edges on the squares remind me very much of the 1970s, and 1980s, when Polaroids were all the rage. (I included a bit of selvedge in the sashing just for fun—just like the photos were.) This quilt's relatively small size makes it easy to quilt on your home sewing machine.

cut the fabric

WOF = width of fabric

From large-scale prints, cut 4 C pieces from each of the 4 fabrics (16 total)

From pink and blue prints, cut 2 B pieces from each of the 8 fabrics (16 total)

From white fabric:

- ○ cut 1 strip 7" × 35½" (18 × 90 cm)
- ○ cut 1 strip 3" × 35½" (7.5 × 90 cm)
- ○ cut 1 strip 8½" × 35½" (21.5 × 90 cm) *
- ○ cut 6 strips 2½" × 14" (6.5 × 35.5 cm)
- ○ cut 16 A pieces

From backing fabric, cut 1 rectangle 40" × 51" (101.5 × 129.5 cm)

From binding fabric, cut 5 strips 2½" (6.5 cm) × WOF

fyi

Fat eighths cut 11" × 18" (28 × 45.5 cm) will also work with this pattern. If you plan on closely spaced quilting as I have done in this project, I recommend adding an extra 2" (5 cm) to the length and width of the backing and batting pieces. Heavy quilting results in more fabric take-up.
* Lastly, if you want to incorporate selvedge into the border, be sure you have prewashed all your fabrics, as selvedges shrink more than the rest of the fabric.

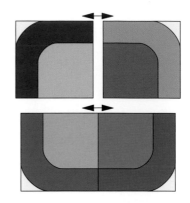

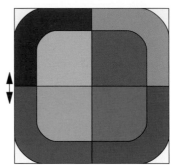

Block Diagram

Make the Block

Because the ends of the A pieces taper to nothing at the edges of the blocks, avoiding raw edges in the finished quilt takes a little maneuvering. Refer to **FIGURE 1** for Steps 1 and 2.

1 Pin an A piece to a B piece, right sides together, matching the centers and the dots at each end of the seam line. Sew the seam between the end dots, backstitching at each dot and leaving the tails of the A piece free. Press the seam allowances toward the A piece (**FIGURE 1**). (See Curved Piecing on page 16 for tips to use while making these blocks.)

2 Matching the center points of the curves, stitch a C piece to the other side of each B piece (**FIGURE 1**). Press the seam allowances toward the B piece. You may find that the seam lies flatter if you clip the seam allowances and press them open.

3 Place the units on your design wall and arrange them in blocks of four units, each block consisting of two units with blue B pieces and two units with pink B pieces. Sew each group of units together as in the **BLOCK DIAGRAM** (see above right), matching seams in the center. Press the seams open. Square the corners of each block if necessary.

Make the Quilt Top

4 Refer to the **CONSTRUCTION DIAGRAM** (see page 128) to complete the quilt top, adding sashing strips as shown: use the 2½" (6.5 cm) strips as vertical sashing between and beside the blocks; use the 3" (7.5 cm) strip between the rows of blocks; use the 7" (18 cm) strip at the top of the quilt; and use the 8½" (21.5 cm) strip at the bottom.

As you sew the sashing strips to the blocks, pay special attention to the points at the ends of the curved seam between pieces A and B.

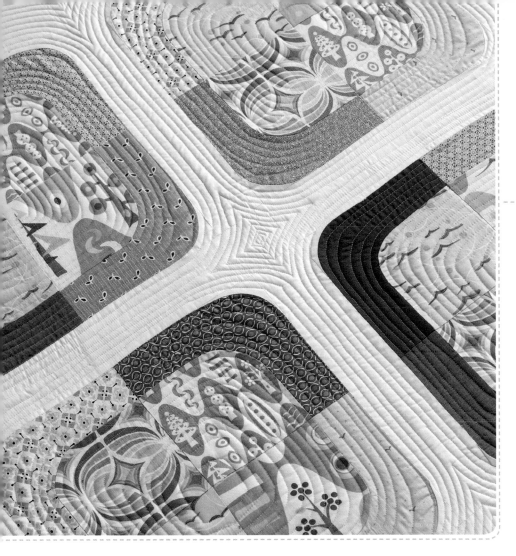

Prints of different scale can be used successfully in a design such as this, where small-scale prints frame the focal blocks.

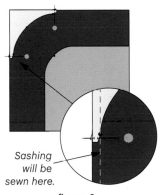

Sashing will be sewn here.

figure 2

Carefully bend the loose ends of each A piece out of the way, into the seam allowance, and pin. Sew precisely across the dot at each end of the seam, keeping the entire block-to-sashing seam straight, without any jogs or pleats **(FIGURE 2)**.

Finish the Quilt

5 This backing needs no assembly, unless you are adding the extra fabric to allow for heavy quilting. If you choose to enlarge the backing, consider piecing the additional width from scraps or purchase extra fabric and cut two pieces 42" (106.5 cm) × WOF.

6 Refer to Finishing Your Quilt (page 18) as needed. Make a quilt sandwich from the backing, batting, and quilt top. Baste all layers together.

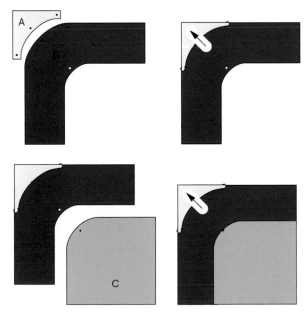

figure 1

7 I used echo quilting to join the layers; I began in the center of a block and finished with three lines of echo quilting outside each large block, with the lines about ¼" (6 mm) apart. I then filled in the empty areas, also echoing those shapes. You may quilt as desired, but I found that this technique accentuated the large blocks. Trim the backing and batting to match the quilt top.

8 Join the 2½" (6.5 cm) binding strips to form a continuous length. Bind the raw edges to finish the quilt.

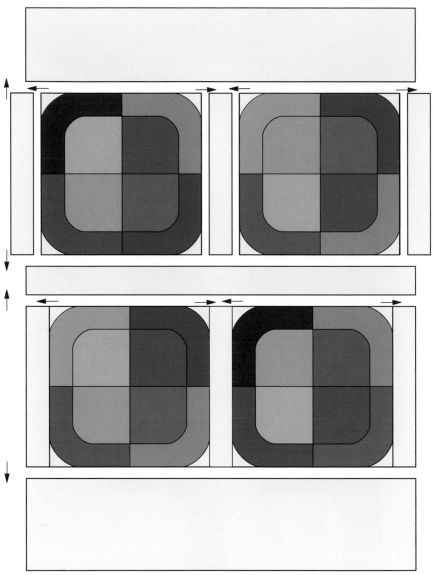

Construction Diagram

I made an easy pieced backing in complementary hues to complete this design.

Resources

While the tools and supplies for the projects in this book can be found easily from local quilt shops, large sewing retailers, and online retailers, here are some of my go-to sources for materials, services, and inspiration.

Fabric, Supplies, and Services

ANDOVER
andoverfabrics.com

ART GALLERY FABRICS
artgalleryfabrics.com

AURIFUL
aurifil.com

BERNINA
bernina.com
A Bernina 710 was used to sew all the quilts in this book.

BIRCH FABRICS
birchfabrics.com

KIM BRADLEY
kimbradleycreations.com

CALICO AND IVY
calicoandivy.com

THE CITY QUILTER
cityquilter.com

CLOTH FABRIC
clothfabric.com

COTTON AND STEEL
cottonandsteelfabrics.com

FABRICWORM
fabricworm.com

FAT QUARTER SHOP
fatquartershop.com

FREESPIRIT
freespiritfabric.com

HAWTHORNE THREADS
hawthornethreads.com

INK AND SPINDLE
lnkandspindle.com

KELANI FABRICS
kelanifabric.com.au

KOKKA FABRICS
kokka.co.jp/en

LIBERTY OF LONDON
liberty.co.uk

MARIMEKKO
marimekko.com

MAZE & VALE
mazeandvale.bigcartel.com

MICHAEL MILLER FABRICS
michaelmillerfabrics.com

MODA FABRICS
storefront.unitednotions.com

NO CHINTZ
nochintz.com

OAKSHOTT FABRICS
www.oakshottfabrics.com

PINK CASTLE FABRICS
pinkcastlefabrics.com

PINK CHALK FABRICS
pinkchalkfabrics.com

PRINTS CHARMING
printscharming.com.au

PURL SOHO
purlsoho.com

SPOTLIGHT
spotlight.com.au

TESSUTI FABRICS
tessuti.com.au

UMBRELLA PRINTS
umbrellaprints.com.au

WINDHAM FABRICS
windhamfabrics.com

Design

ALEXIA ABEGG
alexiaabegg.squarespace.com

AMY BUTLER
amybutlerdesign.com

KRISTEN DORAN
kristendorandesign.blogspot.com

MALKA DUBRAWSKY
stitchindye.com

LEAH DUNCAN
leahduncan.com

FAT QUARTERLY
fatquarterly.com

RITA HODGE
redpepperquilts.com

ANNA MARIA HORNER
annamariahorner.com

KATY JONES
imagingermonkey.blogspot.com

MODERN QUILT GUILD
themodernquiltguild.com

ASHLEY NEWCOMBE
filminthefridge.com

KATIE PEDERSON
sewkatiedid.wordpress.com

DENYSE SCHMIDT
dsquilts.com

LU SUMMERS
blu-shed.blogspot.com

LISA TILSE
theredthread.com

ANGELA WALTERS
quiltingismytherapy.com

VALORI WELLS
valoriwells.com

KRISTA WITHERS
kristawithersquilting.blogspot.com

Art

JOSEF & ANNI ALBERS FOUNDATION
albersfoundation.org

AMERICAN FOLK ART MUSEUM
folkartmuseum.org

MUSÉE D'ORSAY
musee-orsay.fr/en/home

MUSEUM OF CONTEMPORARY ART AUSTRALIA
mca.com.au

MUSEUM OF MODERN ART
moma.org

TATE MODERN
tate.org.uk

VICTORIA AND ALBERT MUSEUM
vam.ac.uk

Artist Biography

Siobhan Rogers is a popular quilting teacher as well as quilt designer in her native Australia. She lives and quilts in Sydney. Her work has appeared in many Australian and international publications, including *Quilter's Companion, Homespun, Down Under Quilts, Fons & Porter's Love of Quilting, Pretty Patches, Fat Quarterly, Studios,* and *Modern Patchwork.*

CONNECT WITH SIOBHAN:

Facebook: Siobhan Rogers
Blog: beaspokequilts.blogspot.com
Pinterest: pinterest.com/beaspokequilts
Twitter: twitter.com/@beaspokequilts
Website: siobhanrogers.com.au
Instagram: instagram.com/
siobhanrogers_beaspoke

INDEX

Find **fresh, colorful projects** and **inspiration**
with these resources from Interweave

VINTAGE QUILT REVIVAL
22 Modern Designs from Classic Blocks

Katie Clark Blakesley, Lee Heinrich, and Faith Jones

ISBN 978-1-62033-054-8
$27.99

IMPROVISING TRADITION
18 Quilted Projects Using Strips, Slices, and Strata

Alexandra Ledgerwood

ISBN 978-1-62033-337-2
$27.99

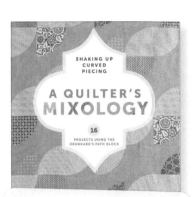

Quilting Daily Shop
Available at your favorite retailer or shop.quiltingdaily.com

Quilting Arts MAGAZINE

Whether you consider yourself a contemporary quilter, fiber artist, art quilter, embellished quilter, or wearable art artist, *Quilting Arts Magazine* strives to meet your creative needs. Quiltingdaily.com

Quilting Daily

Quiltingdaily.com, the online contemporary quilting community, offers free patterns, expert tips and techniques, e-newsletters, blogs, forums, videos, special offers, and more! Quiltingdaily.com